THE
SEXUAL DREAM

THE
SEXUAL DREAM

Joseph M. Natterson, M.D.
AND
Bernard Gordon

CROWN PUBLISHERS, INC. NEW YORK

Printed in the United States of America
Published simultaneously in Canada
by General Publishing Company Limited

Designed by Ruth Kolbert Smerechniak

Library of Congress Cataloging in Publication Data

Natterson, Joseph M
The sexual dream.

1. Sex in dreams.   2. Sex (Psychology)
I. Gordon, Bernard, joint author.   II. Title.
[DNLM: 1. Dreams.   2. Sex.   3. Social problems.
4. Interpersonal relations.   BF1099 S4 N282s]
BF1099.S4N37   1977   155.3   77-8428
ISBN 0-517-53142-9

Contents

II
SEXUAL DREAMS AND INTERPERSONAL PROBLEMS
59

III
SEXUAL DREAMS AND EXISTENTIAL ISSUES
109

IV
THE ART OF THE SEXUAL DREAM
163

cAuthors' Note

Dreaming is dreaming and writing is writing. They are
two very different activities of the human mind. It is not
fully possible to describe a dream in words without color-
ing or distorting the dream, and there is an important reason for this. Language is linear. It is structured. Sentences
march along in organized fashion with subject, predicate
and object, with dependent and independent clauses,
with prepositions and conjunctions. All of this is custom-
ary and necessary to create standards of communication
which will permit the writer or speaker to convey his
meaning as exactly as possible to as many people as possible. But dreams are not primarily verbal. Dreams rely
principally on visual images and frequently on the most

improbable succession of images like those of a motion picture edited by a chimpanzee. So, the effort to relate the dream, to put it into words, sentences, paragraphs, immediately imposes a kind of order on the dream which is alien to it and contradictory to it. Describing a dream is much like trying to describe the Guernica mural to someone who has never seen anything but conventional representational painting, or describing the music of John Cage to someone who has never heard such unstructured sound. There is an abreality to dreams which removes them from the medium of language, and the use of language represents an attempt to cross over from one medium to another as from music or art to literature.

Nevertheless, we are language creatures. Verbal communication is necessary and, whether with regard to Picasso, a modern composer or a dreamer, we continue to use language, however fallibly, to search for meaning and make contact with others.

The dreams in this book have been collected over a period of many years and from a variety of sources. They are presented as nearly as possible in the dreamer's own words. Every dream has been authenticated by the dreamer and changes have been made by the authors only where necessary to protect privacy. But we have imposed even further on the dreamers. Each has read the entire chapter devoted to his or her dreams to verify not merely the accuracy of the dream presentation, but the sense and feeling of the dreams as perceived by the dreamer himself. In this book, all the interpretations of a dream have come from the dreamer or have been corroborated by the dreamer in lengthy personal discussions. In this important sense, each of the dreamers has become a collaborator with the authors in the production of the work and, accordingly, we wish to thank them and dedicate this book to them.

The Dream
and the
Sexual Dream

------•⟨∞⟩•------

We are such stuff
As dreams are made on.
· SHAKESPEARE ·

A mild joke goes back to the early days of popular interest in psychoanalysis. We heard it first in the 1940s. A psychoanalyst, referring to one of his young lady patients, says of her, "The girl is poor and clean but her dreams are rich and dirty." Well, the world was younger then and the joke actually seemed racy to us.

The rise of the sexual dream is a remarkable piece of history. A century ago, the sexual dream was a failed dream because in sexual dreams forbidden wishes erupted into consciousness. In Dostoyevsky's *Crime and Punishment,* Svidrigailov had an openly sexual dream in which a little girl displayed a wanton sexuality toward him. Even

· 1 ·

though he was a wife murderer and sexually quite corrupt, Svidrigailov awakened from this dream in panic and committed suicide. The dream had failed; nineteenth-century man could not face his sexuality.

Now, in the 1970s, overt sexuality is acceptable and the sexual dream has become remarkably useful. It has become a very successful dream form which helps people understand themselves. Today, we are involved in a real sexual revolution, one which concerns a broad reevaluation of the sexual roles of both men and women and which validates the open legitimate status of sex in our culture. Simultaneously, we are witnessing a kind of sideshow which includes a deluge of sex publications, the increasing practice of serial polygamy, urban and suburban switching, group sex, singles bars, X-rated films, porno shops and centerfold nudes which have thrown away the fig leaf and the soft-focus lens. But whether we look to the real revolution or to the sideshow, we find that many people continue to be troubled in their sex lives, troubled by frigidity, impotence, by homosexuality, by incest wishes, by sadism, masochism and guilt. People have problems not only about their sexual behavior but also about their sexual identity. Women can't handle their masculine drives and sometimes confuse these with legitimate strivings for women's liberation. Men cringe and back away from their normal feminine aspect, overcompensate and try to play a ridiculous and destructive *macho* role. Such behavior actually restricts femininity in women and reduces masculinity in men.

It is in dreams that we confront most directly our true sexual inclinations and that we can discover most plainly the sources of our sexual difficulties. But from dreams we can learn a great deal more than this.

Most traditional cultures, whether from Africa, Asia, Europe, the Americas or the Antipodes, accept the premise that dreams are meaningful. The Bible tells of Pharaoh's dream which was interpreted by Joseph and of Nebuchadnezzar's dream which was prophetically understood by Daniel. In your friendly neighborhood supermarket, you can today buy a version of *Zadekial's Book of Dreams and Fortune-Telling* which will inform you that if a maiden dreams of grapes, "this foretells that her husband will be cheerful and a great songster."

Zeno, the stoic philosopher of the third century, B.C., is referred to in a volume of dreams written in 1620: "It was the wise Zeno that said he could collect [understand] a man by his dreams. For then the soul, stated [settled] in a deep repose, bewrayed [revealed] her true affections [feelings]: which in the busy day, she would rather not show or not note. . . . The best use we can make of dreams is observation: and by that, our own correction or encouragement. For 'tis not doubtable, but that the mind is working, in the dullest depth of sleep." (Owen Felltham: "Of Dreams," c. 1620).

Whether we go back to Zeno, back to Joseph and Daniel or further back into the tribal mists of man's beginnings, there is clearly an understanding that dreams tell us a great deal about ourselves. There is endless evidence that man has understood intuitively and well that dreams are meaningful. But it was not until the turn of the twentieth century that Sigmund Freud undertook a systematic approach to the subject with his epochal work on *The Interpretation of Dreams* and built his theories of personality, in large part, on the evidence he discovered in dreams. Though there is ceaseless controversy today on any given detail of Freud's body of work, there is little serious dispute about his conclusion that the dream is the "royal road to the unconscious."

Of course, we concur with Freud about the importance of dreams and with Zeno, the other ancient Greeks, the Hebrews, the Iroquois Indians, the Senoi tribesmen of Malaysia and all the other cultures which have understood that dreams lead us toward truth. We are a bit puzzled about why this extraordinary source of self-knowledge has fallen into relative disuse and even disrepute in our own era just as scientific knowledge about dreams has begun to be available. It's rather as if humanity, which has always been fascinated by the thought of flying, should have abandoned its interest in flight just after the Wright Brothers made their breakthrough at Kitty Hawk.

People today are seeking answers. They are reconsidering religion and considering communes; they are dipping into encounter games, psychedelic stimulation, group therapy, consciousness raising, yoga, transcendental meditation, Hindu and Buddhist mantras, I-Ching and acupuncture. It seems curious that the most ancient, most obvious resource and the one closest to hand, one's own dreams, has been virtually neglected outside of psychoanalysis, as a systematic means of improving self-awareness, reexamining our values and starting on the path of coping with the wildly accelerating changes in the world we know.

Yet it is precisely in the area of sex that dreams play their most direct role. Freud believed that all dreams are sexual. No matter how innocent the manifest content of the dream, Freud discovered that with enough digging into the dreamer's feelings, associations and history, he would come up with a hidden (latent) sexual meaning. Thus, the maiden who dreams so innocently of grapes (manifest content) may, indeed, be dreaming of her lover or future husband as a songster, but when the psychoanalyst encourages her to think deeply about grapes, to associate to their size, shape and texture, she may come up with a meaning that has to do with something quite different from vocal chords.

While we subscribe to Freud's proposition about the latent sexual content of dreams, there is no need to explicate that here; we have a different focus. We wish to deal with dreams that are themselves openly and frankly sexual; everyone has dreams with openly sexual content on occasion. What do such dreams mean? What do they tell us about the dreamer's sexual problems? Do they tell us about more than his or her sexual problems? If a woman has a homosexual encounter in her dream, does that mean she is a homosexual? Does it mean anything else? And what of the man who dreams that the woman he loves has a penis as well as a vagina? It is with such directly sexual dreams that we will primarily concern ourselves because we have learned that the sexual dream is uniquely useful and leads most directly to a consideration of three major areas of the dreamer's life. These are:

1. *The sexual sphere itself.* Direct sexual meanings are revealed in the overt content of the dream and further sexual implications may be discovered in the latent content by a careful study of the dream.

2. *Interpersonal relationships.* The dream will tell us something of the dreamer's relations with his parents, mate, children, brothers, sisters, friends, associates—the entire range of his contacts with other people, his feelings of love and hatred, generosity and greed, selflessness and selfishness, courage and cowardice, honesty and deceit.

3. *Social and political attitudes.* In these dreams, we find mirrored the dreamer's perceptions about the social and cultural world, issues and conflicts such as war, pollution, overpopulation, racism, alienation, democracy, freedom, oppression.

In the sexual dreams we present in this book, we will endeavor to demonstrate how each of the dreams or any series of them touches importantly on all three areas: the sexual, the interpersonal and the socio-political. For example, one of the dreamers has a dream of being raped. This dream has three distinct categories of meaning:

1. (sexual) Her wish for and fear of sexual attack.

2. (interpersonal) Her preoccupation with being exploited by another person when she gets emotionally close.

3. (socio-political) Her rebellious feelings that she is abused as a woman in our male-centered culture, that all authority is threatening, that she and the earth, alike, are being violated by the mindless violence around her.

Our conclusion, after many years of studying dreams, is that the sexual dream is a unique and useful dream form because it gives us the clearest and most direct insight into sexual matters. In the sexual dream, we do not have to decipher obscure symbolism to discover that the knife or the rocket represents a penis; we are dealing with the penis itself. We do not have to dig for the meaning of the purse or the box because the vagina is explicitly represented. Thus, we more readily perceive the overt sexual problem as presented in the dream. And we are given valuable clues to the latent part of the sexual problem. Beyond this, we know that sexual difficulties do not exist encapsulated and separate from the other problems of the individual. A man who suffers from impotence or satyrism will certainly reflect those problems in various ways in other areas of his life. A woman who is troubled by real or imagined homosexual inclinations will be struggling to resolve her feminine identity, her relations with parents, children, marriage, job situation and, perhaps, the role society plays in putting her down.

In dreams without manifest sexual content, the symbols available are without limit. The primitive Eskimo will presumably dream of ice and seals, polar bears, Arctic terns, tools fashioned of bone; the peasant scratching an arid hillside for maize in Mexico will dream of a burro, a cantina, a rural policeman with an automatic rifle; an oil company executive may dream of trans-Atlantic flights, board meetings, dinners with bankers, games with Arabs—whatever. The themes may have something in common but the symbols will come out of the particular life experience of the dreamer. However, when the Eskimo, the peasant and the executive dream overtly of sex, how much variation will they encounter? Human sexual acts and sexual apparatus do not vary much as they appear in dreams. The Senoi tribesman of Malaysia dreams of incest with his sister; how different is that from the incest dream of the attorney from Cincinnati?

Because of the extraordinary forthrightness of the sexual dream, we will concentrate on the presentation of such dreams to demonstrate how they may be analyzed and understood. Since the reader will undoubtedly have his own sexual dreams (especially after his interest in them has been aroused), it will be easier for him to begin to understand his dreams, his sexual and other problems.

Is the understanding of dreams the answer to all your troubles? What about your difficulties with the bill collector, the IRS, Social Security, the price of beans? What about depression, war, the geographic maldistribution of oil? We stop short of claiming cures for such problems. But people who understand themselves better may better understand the world in which they live, and it's well to remember that just as surely as people are shaped by their world, it is also people who react upon and remake that world.

I

SEXUAL
DREAMS
and
SEXUALITY

Incest:
Fire and Ice

Woman may be said to be an inferior man.
· ARISTOTLE ·

Women are only children of a larger growth.
· LORD CHESTERFIELD ·

Woman was God's second mistake.
· NIETZSCHE ·

*Woman is the female of the human species,
and not a different kind of animal.*
· G.B. SHAW ·

LAURA

Sex Lessons from Mother

I am very young again and with the boy I dated when I was
in high school. We are both being aggressively sexual. I
admire the size of his erection, fondle it lovingly, then go
down on him, eagerly taking all of it into my mouth. He is
violent, tries to stuff his penis clear down my throat. Then,
my mother enters the room, watches us go at each other.
My mother is not disapproving but has a mildly pedantic
air. As though she is trying to instruct a couple of playful

kids, she suggests that the boy masturbate in front of us. Then, to demonstrate her meaning, my mother lifts her skirt, bares her vagina and openly and excitedly fingers herself for the benefit of the boy and me. Finally, Mother helpfully orders the boy to have intercourse with me.

Laura reminds us of the girl who was "poor but clean," but with a difference. She is a paragon. A lovely woman, she practices as an attorney and teaches law in a major university. She is married to a successful businessman and is the mother of three fine children. Her father is wealthy and loves her very much and, despite continuing problems with her mother, whom she regards with active hostility, she is keenly aware of her general good fortune and regards it as a trust. She spends much time and energy contributing her legal talent to minority and other underprivileged clients.

During her school years Laura was one of the enviable people who easily achieved top grades and, at the same time, was popular among her fellow students. The major trauma she recalls from those years was the episode when she failed by one or two votes to be elected class president. She returned home from school and wept uncontrollably. Her father slapped her hard. As she recalls it, "He beat me up." Discussing this with him many years later, she found that he denied having done anything more than slap her once to bring her out of her hysterics. In any event, she felt that she had to go out and "win" to get his approval. When she didn't win, she expected an attack. It seems unlikely that he beat her up. But the point is that she felt she merited such violent rejection and though twenty years have passed, she still operates on that premise.

She certainly is a winner. She still gets an "A" in all of her endeavors. She accomplishes without apparent strain what might fatigue half a dozen ordinary people (as wife, mother, attorney, professor, musician, do-gooder and leader in her professional organization). Yet, despite all this, each day is a torment for her. She has developed such an exquisite sense of guilt that she cannot bear to read the daily newspaper. The inevitable accounts of a hungry world, of the oppressed, the disadvantaged, depress her to the point of tears. She cannot reconcile her own affluence and success with the universal pain, misery and hopelessness which each personal contact, each news account reaffirms as the norm for most people in the world.

Though she already accomplishes much, she is a person of protean potential. But she consumes herself with guilt and remorse, not only for the people she might conceivably help but for people so far removed that she could in no way reach them; not only for people but for homeless cats and dogs, for domestic animals led to slaughter, for wild animals hunted and trapped and even for insects fluttering to a painful chemical death.

As a liberated woman, Laura is capable of intense sexual response. But because of her general sense of guilt she contrived to marry a man who would be sexually cold and withholding. Thus she suffers deprivation in her sex life which is clearly related to the pain she experiences in the other spheres of feeling. Laura wishes to change all this.

What does the dream disclose? Uninvited and uninstructed, she goes down on the boy. Though this is a form of sexual pleasure very commonly enjoyed by women, it is also frequently regarded as low behavior and less permissible than the genital sex act itself. The fact that she indulges herself so freely in the dream expresses Laura's wish to free herself of the sexual strictures and guilt she cannot shake off when in bed and awake. The fact that Momma is there assisting and instructing her helps to bolster her conviction that such behavior is socially acceptable.

Why does she add to the scenario that the boy tries to choke her with his penis? For one thing, it suggests that her sexual behavior is so exciting that her partner is maddened with desire and out of control. This is a pleasing fantasy for a sexually deprived woman. Insofar as the boy's behavior is unpleasant or threatening, we may assume that the censor is still at work telling Laura that even as she indulges in libidinous dreams, she may yet gag on her own appetite.

In actuality, the mother was prudish and sexually enfeebled. The daughter in the dream is not only parodying her mother for whom she had good reason to feel hostility, but she is expressing a deeply felt wish that her mother had been sexually free and could have enjoyed her own body; thus, she might not have programmed her own sexual limitations onto her daughter. Girls identify with their mothers in sexual matters. Laura, however unwillingly, patterned her own sexual attitudes after her mother's and, despite a totally different social, moral and religious outlook, cannot completely shake off the mother's prudery.

Laura who, in her waking life is so paralyzed with feelings of guilt that she literally cannot kill a fly, dreams of participating in a sex circus that would sell tickets in Tijuana—and with her mother! There is, here, a clear attempt to work through the sexual repression, related to the mother, so as to be able to cope with her adult sexual limitations. By including her mother in the dream of sexual liberation, Laura is also touching on areas of personal relations, areas of intimacy, that go beyond the purely sexual. How does she feel about her mother as a woman? How does she perceive her mother's lifelong influence on her, the daughter, in value areas that go beyond sexual behavior and into broader questions of guilt and liberation? How much does she blame her mother for loading her with the problems that plague her in her everyday life? Why does Laura, in her dream, perceive the mother in terms of cruel and licentious parody, a great put-down, unless she is trying to vomit out a lifetime of repression for which she largely blames her mother?

Laura has other dreams which express her attempts to liberate herself sexually. She dreams that she has left her front door unlocked. A neighbor (who exists in reality and whom she regards as virile and attractive) appears in the dream and tells her that it is obvious, from the unlocked door, that she has a lover.

The unlocked door is a charming and typical symbol of the receptive female sex organs just as "going in the back door" is common jargon for anal penetration. In her little dream about the unlocked door and the observant neighbor, it appears that Laura has moved her fantasies up from the high school level to the present and is toying pleasantly with the notion of a sexual encounter with the real live one who lives next door.

While any dream, even such a fragment as this, may be endlessly analyzed for layers of meaning, it is enough for now to note that Laura is continuing her struggle to unlock her sexual potential. Whatever her other problems, it is clear from her dreams that it is in the area of sex that Laura presently feels most keenly deprived. Her dreams reveal more than this as we see in her next dream.

Father and the Four-Letter Word

Laura works in a law firm where the senior partner is an extremely attractive man of mature years. He is warm, charming, supportive, paternal. She feels a filial devotion to him and knows, regretfully, that he would never mix business with pleasure by making a pass at her. She dreams:

> The boss and I are together for an assignation in another city. We are presumably in a hotel room and we are both eager for sex. But the man refuses to touch me unless I state categorically—and in so many words—that "I want you to fuck me." Of course, I am most reluctant to speak this way before the senior partner but he is adamant and I force myself to say the words. I don't recall the sex act which presumably followed but, as in an X-rated film edited for television, I next recall some fussing about the luggage. It seems the boss is arranging to leave our bags in this distant city so that we will have an excuse to repeat the rendezvous. I, however, am not at all certain that I want a return engagement.

Clearly, the senior partner—in life and in the dream—is an authority figure, a surrogate father. Laura, in this dream, is able to face the fact so flimsily concealed, that she has harbored incestuous desires for her father. It has been remarked by almost all observers since Freud that young children are sexually polymorphous. It is probably safe to go further and say that young children, before the taboos are fixed, are equally curious sexually about dogs, cats, canaries and Teddy bears, as they are about momma, poppa, brother and sister. But with sexual roles stereotyped early in our culture, it is even more true that a girl will look to the strongest male figure on her horizon as an appropriate sex object. It is normal; it is inevitable for a girl to have sexual feelings for her father; and just as inevitably she will feel guilty about this.

Incest is a subject of consuming interest throughout human history. It has been forbidden almost universally and practiced with social sanction only rarely as in the case of certain Egyptian Pharaohs (brother and sister) where, possibly, the incest proved that they were above the law and really set apart from all the rest of common mortals. Indeed, they were regarded as gods, and gods have notoriously indulged in sexual hijinks. But for the rest of us commoners today, we must accept that incest is frowned upon; we must repress such desires, encounter them only in dreams and, above all, feel guilt because we ever had such feelings—or continue to have them.

In the last dream, above, Laura is not only engaging in a sexual liaison with a father surrogate, but she quite clearly betrays the true identity of her dream lover in the passage where the man insists that she speak the forbidden words if she wants his sexual favors. Who but a father would make an issue of the words she may or may not use? If we know anything about the real senior partner of this law firm, he'd much prefer to cloak the whole affair in tender and romantic language—and so would Laura (whose dream it is). Someone with great authority is on the scene, a teacher, a guide, a first and final father figure. Surely it's daddy himself. She must obey him and she does. Thus, it appears that still, as an adult in her thirties, a wife and mother, she has quite specific though unconscious sexual drives toward her father. Her continuing incestuous wishes and her fierce struggle to repress them explain two of the outstanding characteristics of this unusual woman: First, she habitually denies herself sexual gratification as a form of punishment for her forbidden wishes; second, she typically subordinates her wishes to others, works compulsively to do "good," gets high marks in all her endeavors and experiences an exaggerated concern for the welfare of others to compensate for her own guilt feelings.

While dreams of incestuous wishes and activities are commonplace, the central feature of this dream is unusual and refreshing. The man's firm demand that she put her wishes into unambiguous words sounds like an inner voice saying: "All right, face it. You want your father to fuck you. Don't mince words. Don't speak euphemistically of incest, instinctual drives and all the rest of the jargon with which you dress up and conceal the real emotional impact of your feelings. If you say the true words; if you will tell your father, 'I want us to fuck,' only then will you face the full reality, bring it all out into the open, feel it in your gut and be able to examine its true meaning." Then, after she does say the words, the dream leaps over the sexual scene and moves to the problem of the luggage! The man, it seems, wants to continue the liaison. But, now, Laura is not certain that she wants it. It's as though the words, the full and undiluted statement of truth in the dream, is an incantation which has freed Laura, at last, of her incestuous drive.

Laura continues to dream:

Pandora's Purse

> I've never been in the Hugh Hefner pad in Chicago or even seen pictures of it but this house in my dream was about what I imagined it to be—crazy Victorian, Art Nouveau

mixed with Modern, the old dark house of British horror films, Mary Shelley played by Jane Fonda, curlicue banisters, stairways leading to meaningless landings, whorehouse red plush draperies, lots of brass and cut glass mixed with chrome and plastic. There's an orgy going on all over this wild place and, though I recall no specifics at the beginning, I know I am sexually aroused. Then I am in a smaller room and simultaneously notice that men are entering several rooms like the one I'm in. With terror, I realize they are killing people like me. First I hide in a closet and then I try to run out of the house but they catch me despite my furious resistance. In the midst of this frenzied fear, I calmly open my purse—as though the danger has suddenly evaporated. I observe several condoms in the purse and I feel very foolish for checking on contraceptives when I have just narrowly escaped death. In this portion of the dream, I oscillate between a feeling that I am a man and the feeling that I am a woman.

This dream converges sharply on the issue of Laura's chronic sexual frustration. In the dream she sees men running around freely in this *Playboy* world, taking whatever pleasures they wish: sexual, even murderous. But it is women, like her, who must suffer and even die at the hands of the men. An alternative, then, is to be a man. They, unlike women, can enjoy sex without inhibiting guilt. So, in the dream, her wishes to be male are revealed.

The most explicit image in the dream is the one of Laura opening her purse in the midst of the frenzy and observing the condoms inside. A purse is probably the most widely recognized Freudian symbol for the vagina. Though we reject any mechanical approach which dictates that a purse or anything else invariably symbolizes a given object, the purse in this dream occurs like a textbook example of the Freudian thesis. In this dream of manic sex, Laura opens her purse and sees the condoms. Opening the purse, then, can mean opening herself genitally in the midst of the orgy so that she can participate in the sexual activity. For Laura, it is a courageous act to try to open herself sexually in the midst of so much frightening mas-

culine aggression. What does she get for her pains? She
finds the condoms. To have condoms in one's possession
is the act of someone who has made plans for sexual
pleasure or, at least, for sexual encounter. She says in her
dream, "I feel foolish for checking on contraceptives when
I have just narrowly escaped death." She is saying that
death and terror and brutal aggression are so prevalent in
this world that it is morally wrong (foolish) to think about
planning for sexual pleasure.

In her dream, Laura is rationalizing her feelings of sexual deprivation, telling herself that sex is not so important,
that she can live without it. She concludes her account of
the dream by saying, "In this portion of the dream, I oscillate between feeling that I am a man and feeling that I am a
woman." She appears to be saying, now, that the answer
to her problems may be to be a man, live like a man. We
already know enough about Laura to understand that in
her career and her social life, she is aggressive and competitive with men in their own usual bailiwick of professional
endeavor. So, it is not surprising to see the masculine-
feminine identity issue come out explicitly in the dream.
But it may be helpful for Laura to see forcefully, via the
dream, that she wants to identify with those creatures
who fling themselves at the world aggressively, taking
what they want in terms of career and creative satisfac-
tions, even killing when they choose, and all without any
feelings of guilt.

From a social point of view, it is clearly valid for a woman to wish to reject the limitations placed on her activities and potentials by a traditional male-centered society.
But, in her dream, this is not what Laura is reaching for.
She is not saying that as a matter of common sense and
justice she is going to insist on equal rights professionally
or otherwise; no, she is trying to unload her deep feelings
of guilt and sexual inadequacy. She appears to be thinking
that to be a man in this world is to be free of all such problems. As a sophisticated person she knows that in the real
world, real men do suffer from guilt, sexual deficiency, in-

ability to cope with feelings of aggression and the entire gamut of problems which are familiar to her as a woman. But her dream reveals that inside her, where it counts, she has not yet gotten it straight and she continues to envy men and wishes to emulate them for the wrong reasons. If she does get it straight, she will not want to be a man, not be confused about whether it is better to be a man or a woman. She will want to be a woman who can enjoy sex without the strictures of guilt and, too, a woman who is free to function in the world without the barriers created by "male chauvinist pigs."

Laura's sexual dreams clue us in very clearly to her problems of sexuality. They demonstrate her wish to be freer sexually; they express her continued struggle to liberate herself of guilt at the level of her incestuous drives toward her father; they disclose a problem of sexual identity which is central to many of her other problems. Her dreams also explore her attitudes toward her mother and father, attitudes which are basic in forming the intimate interpersonal relationships she makes through life with friends, lovers, husband, children, siblings, associates. Finally, her dreams vividly portray Laura's perception of the brutal and painful male-oriented world in which she lives and help to explain her daily preoccupation with the exploitation and injustice she sees everywhere. A healthier Laura would feel no less indignant but would tackle the problems she perceives with gusto and even greater effectiveness.

𝒫remature 𝒠jaculation

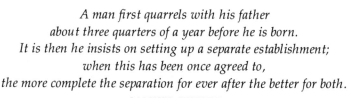

A man first quarrels with his father
about three quarters of a year before he is born.
It is then he insists on setting up a separate establishment;
when this has been once agreed to,
the more complete the separation for ever after the better for both.
· SAMUEL BUTLER ·

JOHN

Johnny Come Quickly

My two sisters are in a large double bed. There is an orange-beige quality to the room, suggesting the mass-produced tastelessness of Las Vegas, although the locale is never made explicit. I am standing at one side of the bed and I am with another person, probably a man. We are about to carry out some plan, perhaps criminal or just possibly cruel and immoral but in the service of a surpassingly noble cause. I am horrified that in order to carry out our

· 21 ·

plot, it is necessary to kill my sisters with a knife or a pistol or a needle; the exact nature of the lethal instrument is not clear. My sister nearer to where I am standing has her head covered, probably feigning sleep; earlier she had been awake but offering no protest or resistance. On the one hand, I feel capable of the murder, but on the other, I feel deep love for my sisters. I empathize with the sister who is awake and yet is willing to be killed rather than be difficult. I am horrified, filled with self-loathing and feel I cannot harm them. My other sister has slept soundly throughout the entire scene.

Then the locale and cast of characters change. However, I am again in a hotel; this time, though, the corridors and public rooms have a huge cavernous quality. A large convention may be in progress. Some of my married friends have paired me with a celebrated beauty; I am somewhat surprised that she is heavier than one would expect. She and I have apparently just had intercourse, and I realize she is angry, cold and hostile toward me. It then dawns on me that I must have come too quickly, leaving her sexually aroused but frustrated. She and I are talking about this as we walk through the convention area. This part is vague but I recall that we walked through the rear portions of rooms with hundreds or thousands of people in attendance. There is about the scene something similar to the halls of the United Nations where plenary sessions are held. However, these meetings seem unimportant to me; I am anxious, ashamed of my sexual inadequacy. I start to tell the woman that I will try to give her sexual satisfaction, e.g., cunnilingus enters my mind, but I quickly realize that this would be futile appeasement and I don't mention it. I don't want to compound the felony and appear even more foolish. The dream ends on this unsatisfactory note.

John is forty-five years old and married. He is a journalist who is locally prominent and nationally recognized; but to his chagrin, he is not really big league and only sporadically creative. He is very ambitious and knows enough to realize there are some sinister roots to his ambition; it isn't all just good old Protestant ethic. He suffers that he has not fulfilled his ambitions, although most men would gladly trade places with him in his success and prosperity. Also, he suffers from the symptoms of premature ejaculation. In his work, he is certainly successful, but not outstanding. In the bedroom, he performs adequately but he is no stud. He has similar feelings about both situations.

John comes from a Midwestern family. During the Twenties, his father had a prosperous business, but when the Great Depression caught him, he never recovered. John has one sister a couple of years older and one sister a year younger than he. With considerable deprivation, the family squeaked through the 1930s. They were decent people but poverty and shabbiness induced an ambience of resentment toward one another, shame for themselves and intense compensating fantasies of freer and fuller lives. John and his younger sister were able to scrounge through college and professional school, make their way in the world and make tracks as far as possible from Main Street and Middletown.

John woke from the dreaming somewhat uncomfortable with his self-portrayal, first as a cruel sister-killer, then as a sexual weakling incapable of handling a real woman. But he quickly enough saw the amusing side of the dream; at least, no one could accuse him of being pompous or self-glorifying. Taking a first broad look at the dream, one might reach the following conclusion: the dream of sex trouble with the "celebrated beauty" expresses a wish to have more staying power, i.e., not to come so quickly when he makes love to his wife and to feel more solid and important in his profession.

But what of the dream about his sisters? Overtly, the relationship with his sisters was most agreeable, but this did not conform to deeper truths. John had always resented them; as a child he had even wished them dead. The motives for these fantasies were petty, at least on a conscious level: fundamentally, he yearned for a fresh start in a rich, powerful and established family. He resented being tied to the grubby existence his sisters personified. Recalling the first part of the dream, the two women in the bed and the two men plotting their death . . . what does it mean? Why is John so deviously determined to murder the sleeping sisters? In trying to associate to the dream, John had a sudden recollection that his father had had a petty, sneaky streak which had always galled John. But sons inevitably identify with their fathers, so we may assume that John detected some of these same vile traits in himself; he resented them and blamed his father for them. Then came a shocker: he now recalled that many years earlier, his older sister had told him that when John was four or five years old, his father and an equally impoverished friend had become desperadoes, had ineptly robbed a store, were caught and probably served a little time. The violent events of those early days, so long forgotten, undoubtedly had made a profound impression on John.

Now it was coming clearer. John felt he was a criminal—like his father. But to be a criminal, one must be guilty of crimes. What were John's crimes? Since, as a successful journalist, he had never had occasion to stick up a drugstore, he had to pin his "criminal" behavior or tendencies onto something. For those of us who want to feel guilty about something (and who doesn't?), incestuous wishes are available and infallible. For John, bracketed by two sisters, it was easy. Add to this his "death wishes," i.e., his hostility to the shabby background they represented, and we have a good case for convicting John as a sister-screwing murderous s.o.b. John had carried within himself all these years a need to be like his father (every son does) and actually embrace as a fundamental part of his personality the very "furtive criminal" facade which, on a conscious level, he loathed in his father. Using incest and death wishes, so common to all of us, as convenient hooks, he had succeeded in achieving his own criminal identity, a parody of his father's.

We can go further into the matter of "criminality" by recalling the reference in the dream to the "halls of the United Nations." As a journalist, John is concerned with writing the truth about world affairs. He has an active social conscience. But he must also serve the editors and publishers who pay for his comfortable and exciting life-style. Does John feel, perhaps, that he pulls his punches, sells out the truth just a trifle to assure his continued professional position? Is he guilty of opportunism, a "crime" of considerable dimensions where the very future of the world is at stake as in the deliberations of the United Nations? If John wants to portray himself as a criminal he will, no less than the rest of us, find sufficient grounds.

But what has all this to do with premature ejaculation? Well, if there's one thing John could tell us from his early reading of Street and Smith crime stories, it is that a criminal is usually on the lam. He has to grab his pleasures where he can and make tracks because the cops, the private eyes or the other white hats are always close behind. A petty criminal (and we're not talking of Fu Manchu) is not a relaxed voluptuary. He has to act quickly and move on. John's uneasy and pervading sense of guilt, his unsettled feeling that "they" will catch up with him if he settles down to one pleasure, to one task, has made it impossible for him fully to pleasure himself in sex or fully to exploit any of his considerable talents. This pattern of hit-and-run, skating on surfaces, keeping on the move, has limited his effectiveness all the way from the nuptial bed to the editorial pages of a national magazine.

From the first stab at explaining John's dream as a wish to have more staying power with both his wife and his work, we have moved on to deepen our understanding of the dream and also of the roots of the problem. Certainly, it was useful for the dream to remind John that he is dissatisfied with his performance both sexually and professionally; but that much would not be much help, not really deepen the man's insight. Now, reviewing the implications of the dream, John could begin to understand the sources of his difficulties in his childhood attitudes toward his sisters and in his need (for which he hated himself) to ape his father's weaker self. For the first time, he could see that he carried around this image of himself as a criminal and that much of his self-depreciation flowed from this. He could see more clearly, too, why the pattern of his sexual behavior (hop on and hop off) was echoed in his social and professional life.

For John, the lifelong criminal, there is much more that remains unexplained in his dream. Exactly who is the overweight beauty whom he has disappointed in the hay? Who is the shadowy male companion in the hotel room murder scene? Why the pointed reference to the "rear" of the conference room? Why is he introduced to the beauty by "married" friends? Since every element of the dream scenario was invented by John, we can safely assume that every element has some meaning. But no single dream need be explored forever to yield every last drop of substance. If John learns to overcome the fugitive sense which keeps him frantically on the run, he may yet go back to explore this same dream with additional profit. Meanwhile, though, this sexual dream has shed light on the nature and origin of his sexual difficulties and on the profound relationship between his sexual conduct and all his other behavior.

Few secrets are guarded so jealously as a man's own feeling of sexual inadequacy. A man listens to locker room talk of conquest and sexual athleticism, boasts of rock-hard erections that last for hours and bring the girl to climax two, three or more times in succession (usually lies). A man joins the talk but compares himself unfavorably with the presumed paragons of virility, the movie stars, athletes and the muscle-bound type next door who tunes up his own car and swills beer from the can. An ordinary man with the ordinary burden of sexual problems feels inferior and the feeling of inferiority bleeds over into every area of endeavor. Premature ejaculation is very common in our culture and a source of much agony for the men who feel sexually inadequate, unsatisifed, crippled. Are all such cases, like John's, a result of identifying with a "criminal" father? Of course not. But guilt in any of its many forms, alienation from one's work or career and a confused identification with an imperfect father are indeed common denominators among us. Only your own dreams can pinpoint the exact source of your own difficulties.

Frigidity

Her heart, be sure, is not of ice.
· BYRON ·

MAXINE

Shit. *Merde. Mierda. Dreck.* In the languages of human society, the word for excrement is an epithet. It denotes something nasty, repulsive. Even the reader of these words may react with annoyance. Is it really necessary to be so crude, so provocative, so obvious to achieve effect? As something that is always swept under the rug, or more properly, flushed down the toilet with guilty haste, it is certainly time to lift the lid on the subject. For shit (or our attitude toward it) appears importantly in our dreams and is often associated with serious problems of sexual behavior.

Is this strictly a contemporary phenomenon, or is it timeless? What do we know of the treatment of the bowel movement in other cultures? We have reason to believe that the more sophisticated and complex a culture, the more concern there is about baby having an accident on the living-room floor. After all, it's easier to clean up the trodden earth of a wickiup than an Aubusson carpet. We do know that the ancient Romans were diligent in their construction of sewers and justifiably proud of the result. But, because of the perishability of the material, there is little that remains for the anthropologist to find. Bones, tools, kitchen middens, burial grounds—yes. But where are the turds of long ago? And, more important, how did *Pithecanthropus erectus* really feel about his stool?

Is our present attitude toward excrement an outgrowth of capitalism, feudalism, primitive communism? Lewis Henry Morgan and Friedrich Engels indulged in fascinating conjecture about latter-day attitudes toward such basic subjects as women and marriage, associating them with the rise of agriculture, the settling on private property, the desire of a father to pass on his land and cattle to offspring he was certain were his own. They explored women's subjugation in class and property terms a hundred years before Gloria Steinem could read "Little Bo-peep." But not a single word about feces.

Is the problem inherent in the human psyche? Does it arise like the opposable thumb and the development of language to differentiate us from the lower animals? If "Mama" was the first word uttered by man, was "shit" the second?

While we are aware that healthy animals do not "foul" their own nests, dens, lairs, we also witness dogs determinedly sniffing turds along the curb, showing no sign of aversion—only an anxious over-the-shoulder glance toward a sourly disapproving mistress who is about to yank hard on the leash. Though, regrettably, our city streets are no longer sprinkled with fragrant horse manure, some of us can recall as children watching with fascination as sparrows enthusiastically rooted around in the dung for undigested grain or whatever it is that city birds found in horse– – – –.

Maxine is exceptionally attractive, highly educated, well-married and successful in her career. Her only problem is that she is frigid.

When she was in her early infancy, her father and mother separated. Subsequently the father made no serious effort to develop a relationship with her, although he lived in a nearby city and she was his only daughter. At parochial school, Maxine was terrified by the nuns' primitive religiosity, and from early childhood she feared defecating because of a conviction that a witch would emerge from the toilet and pull her down into the netherworld. She became a precocious, cute, bratty type who managed her mother and her mother's immature lover.

She grew into a prim and sober woman who was exceptionally competent in her profession of nursing and rapidly climbed into the supervisorial ranks—always managing people. She married "out of the faith," a sympathetic and puritanical Prostestant boy who was shy and unaggressive though brilliant in his field of industrial chemistry. He needed a mothering type and was fortunate to find a girl who was lovely, successful in her own work, and so eager to run everything for both of them—including their sex life.

But there was always one problem. Though she loved her husband, she could not achieve orgasm in intercourse, nor with masturbation (which she rarely tried because it was so messy and nasty), nor in her dreams which were mostly repressed but which never, to her recollection, reached sexual climax.

Maxine, though she started out with a parochial background, long left that behind. With a master's degree in her field from a top university, with many courses in psychology, she knows "all about" sex, orgasm, anal eroticism, the works. She can even give useful counsel in sexual matters though, true to her stringent moral code, she feels hypocritical when she does this.

Sometime after her marriage, Maxine resumed her postgraduate studies and became collaboratively involved with an older professor. The man was mature, understanding, professionally helpful and did not try to exploit her sexually. When she was able, finally, to confide some of her problems to him, he tried to counsel her. Maxine, of course, realized that this man was like a father to her, the "good father" she had so bitterly missed and she began to believe that through this relationship she might work out some of her emotional blocks, relinquish her great need to control and, not so incidentally, achieve orgasm.

An American Rope Trick

Well along in the relationship with the older man, Maxine had this dream:

> The professor and I are having intercourse on a bed. We are literally locked in a copulating embrace because we are tightly bound together by dark brown rope an inch or more thick. I cannot move although I would like to. A door opens into a dimly lit bathroom in which I can see a sink, a mirror and the toilet. I am very aware of the bathroom.

As she thought about the dream, Maxine recalled that, in it, she felt as though she were being held captive. She was especially conscious of having been afraid to move —which she interpreted as being afraid to respond sexually, to come. The hairy ropes reminded her of pubic hair, of being smothered in pubic hair, of being burned by rubbing against a rope. At the same time, the constricting rope engendered a safe, comfortable feeling; she knew it prevented her from falling off the bed.

But what of the bathroom and the prominent toilet in her view all the while she engaged in intercourse? What of the brown-colored rope an inch or more thick? Surely, here, we are dealing with that old toilet problem. "Afraid to move" most likely does mean "afraid to come." But it also means "afraid to have a movement of the bowels," a common enough construction in our language.

And exactly what was "holding her captive"? Pubic hair? Perhaps. But Maxine had never gotten involved enough to be "held captive" by anything pubic. More likely, we are dealing with that four-letter word, shit, the nasty stuff she has been holding onto since she was a small child when the evil witch might come up from the toilet, get her and drown her in all the shit down there (along with the evil-smelling brimstone promised her by the nuns). Of course, the pubic, i.e., the sexual thing, was all mixed up in it as inescapably as the anal and sexual orifices are situated in such confusing proximity.

Maxine's fear from an early age of "letting go" her stool was a fear of opening herself up emotionally on any level, including opening herself up to a penetrating penis; there was the fear from childhood of being rejected and wounded as she had evidently been by the loss of her father. In later life, this became a fear of coming, an inability to lose herself in the ecstasy of orgasm which would have meant a loss of control; it would have meant handing over to someone else, a man, the power over her pleasure; better to do without than risk that. Since Maxine could not trust her well-being to any other person, she achieved her sense of security by controlling others: her mother, her mother's lover, her husband, friends, patients and her subordinates in the medical complex.

Now that she had built a relationship with a "good father," an older man who would not exploit her or abandon her, Maxine could dream of a sexual encounter which had elements of satisfaction even though it did not yet achieve climax.

The dream gave her material for thought at a time when through study, honest digging into her own problems and increasing maturity, she could begin to understand and use the message from her unconscious: the combination of sexual activity and the hard persistent porcelain image of the toilet was a useful juxtaposition; the duality of being chained and confined by the "ropes" yet given a sense of security by them was another clue; the ambiguity of the pubic hair and shit was certainly suggestive and pointed down a useful path.

But perhaps the word "ambiguity" is wrong. We are not dealing here with a lack of clarity and definition but rather a marvelous poetic compression. The subject matter may not suggest poetry but shit and pubic hair are both appropriate to the dreamer's problem and are combined in a single dramatic symbol; ropes which enslave but offer security are, again, a creative fusion; sexual activity with an eye on the toilet brings together what appear superficially to be disparate subjects. Poetry is the creation of meaningful images; it is the use of compression in language to convey meaning with the fewest words; it is the communication of our deepest feelings through the manipulation of vivid symbols. This dream, like so many others, illustrates the relationship of dream language to the language of poetry. It helps explain why folk wisdom couples the poet and the dreamer. It suggests that the poet (writer, artist, creative worker in any field) is the one who has better access to his dreams and his unconscious. And this brings into focus our belief that all of us, if on better terms with our dreams, might live richer and more creative lives.

Maxine? Remember that she was a person who throughout her lifetime had practiced rigid self-control and had arranged her life so as to manage all those around her, men and women both. In the easy psychological jargon of our day, she would be called an emasculator or a ball-cutter. But she was also a person of exceptional integrity who worked hard to dig through the endless confusion and false trails laid down by the unconscious. And she was lucky. She met someone who could help her when she was ready for help. The compression of images in Maxine's dream, the binding fecal ropes fused with sexual intercourse, suggest a transition from seeking security through holding on too tightly to finding security in a trusting relationship with another person, the man who is making love to her in the dream. In fact, it was shortly after this dream and her rigorous appraisal of it that she began having orgasm in masturbation. This was, of course, no mere nervous, muscular and glandular response to physical manipulation. It was a hundred-and-eighty-degree turn in direction for a courageous woman who had felt crippled by a serious handicap which extended into all areas of living. Almost another year passed but then, happily, she began to achieve orgasm with her husband.

It has been remarked that when the infant delivers his first stool into the potty, he is praised, loved and rewarded by his grateful mother who is overanxious about bowel function and is most happy to be finished with the messy diaper routine. The normal infant naturally gets the notion that his stool is a valuable gift to his all-important mother and rightfully regards it as a pearl of great price. Try to conceive Junior's chagrin when, a moment later, he sees it flushed down the toilet with obvious aversion. What can he conclude?

While this supremely intimate moment between mother and child is not usually celebrated in soft-focus calendar art, nor used by Norman Rockwell for a magazine cover on Mother's Day, it is certainly one of the more important events in a child's development. It is important, not so much in itself, but because it is representative of countless thousands of other encounters between the child and his mother, father, siblings and all the other figures who influence him, exercise control over him and force him to control himself during his earliest and most responsive years.

The thrust of the process is something like this: the child's body produces stools and the child must get rid of them; the mother, in our Western machine-oriented society, finds the stools offensive; at a very early age (too early), the mother enforces control over the child (by punishment and withholding love) if the child continues to defecate in inconvenient places; the child is required to learn to control his own body functions at too early an age; the need for too much self-control at a premature age contributes to anxiety, a loss of his sense of freedom and spontaneity, a loss of self-love and love for others, of creativity and, ultimately, of his ability to respond sexually in his later years.

Of course, we do not mean that the scene on the potty chair and the extension of this into the area of anal control is the only cause for such problems. In a given individual, it may not even be the main cause. But the chain of events we describe is one of the important causes of personality difficulty in a culture where premature control and an aversion for natural functions work together to distort the performance and the values of the developing individual.

Values enter into the equation because, going back to the archaic scene, mother was pleased by the child's performance but she clearly disliked the nasty stuff. The child wonders: Is it good? Or is it bad? Is it possible for something to be both good and bad? Why does mother want him to produce the stool, praise him for the act, coo encouragingly at his performance but in virtually the same breath reject him for this same product? Why is mother ambivalent about the damned thing? The concept of ambivalence is, of course, beyond the child but ambivalence is at the very heart of our culture: we glorify the machine which destroys nature and, in virtually the same breath, sentimentalize and glorify nature. On Sunday, we elevate the Christian ethic of "Love thy neighbor" and, on the other six days of the week, we urge Junior to compete like hell against his neighbor whether it's in the ball park or on the way to the bank.

What's good? What's bad? Is that turd in the pot a prize or is it something nasty? Do we hold it in or "let it all hang out?" That confusing moment with his mother is going to come back to haunt Junior on many levels. And the adult confusion and conflict of values will frequently be symbolized in his dreams by toilets, defecation, feces, brown and binding ropes, because that's where it all began, that's where the pattern of ambivalence was first encountered.

It's too bad that so many important things are going to be confused with something which is not intrinsically important. Now, the secret is out. Shit is neither good nor bad. Ask your dog. Ask an eagle. It is just another thing like a leaf or a stone. Only thinking makes it important. In our culture. Whether it is perverted into something more or less important to the worshippers of Shiva in India or the followers of Mao in China is a question that bears serious investigation. Meanwhile, though, in the hygienic U.S.A. and in the other advanced Western industrialized societies that try to follow running water to Utopia, you may be certain that in blatant or disguised form, you're going to meet your feces in your dreams. Don't turn up your nose. This may be a most valuable clue offered to you in relation to any number of problems. Treat this stool as spoor—treat it with the objective sanity of any healthy predator on the trail of a succulent reward.

A sex dream, a dream of copulation, has led us into an examination of the frigidity of the dreamer, of the toilet training traditions of our culture, of the intimate and intense interpersonal relationships which dominate the dreamer's life and a glancing look at our values regarding love, sex, ambition, success. Maxine's perceptions of all these areas are closely linked with her history of sexual repression. Her sexual dreams are helping her to define her sexual problems and will help her to explore other matters of friendship, work and personal attitudes in the broadest social context.

Homosexual Conflict

---··⟨∞⟩··---

I wander through each charter'd street
  Near where the charter'd Thames does flow,
And mark in every face I meet
  Marks of weakness, marks of woe.

In every cry of every Man,
  In every Infant's cry of fear,
In every voice, in every ban,
  The mind-forg'd manacles I hear.
              · WILLIAM BLAKE ·

MARK

The Uncircumcised Faucet

I am in a bathhouse that is like a charnel house. I am being forced to suck the penis of an uncircumcised man. The penis is like a faucet.

Mark, a man in his late twenties, is energetic and imaginative, a creative artist. For years he has been struggling against his homosexuality, which conflicts with his wish to marry, establish a family and settle down to a conventional

· 36 ·

life-style. We are not concerned here with the psychology of homosexuality, *per se*, but rather with homosexual dreams for the light they may shed on the sexual attitudes and conflicts of the dreamer, whether a man or a woman, homosexual or not.

It is important to remember that the above dream occurred to a man who, while overtly homosexual, was struggling against this behavior. Sophisticated, member of an international set, Mark was not in conflict with his homosexuality on narrow provincial moralistic grounds. But he did have other conflicts.

Examining some of the specifics of the dream, we find Mark is "in a bathhouse that is like a charnel house." The dream seems to say that his sexual impulses lead him into a bleak and frightening environment. In life, the men he finds sexually attractive, the men he will pick up for sexual encounters in bars and on street corners, are physically strong but intellectually and culturally barren, devoid of moral concerns. To Mark, they are frightening people who inhabit a menacing world, a chamber of horrors—a charnel house.

He is "forced to suck the penis of an uncircumcised man." Since he is "forced," he sees himself in this dream as a victim, unwillingly engaging in the homosexual act. Further, the penis is uncircumcised. Mark, a Jew, betrays in his dream a sense of persecution. The partner is a Gentile, a brute, a "goy" who preys upon Mark's sensitivity and weakness. Further, the penis is "like a faucet." Presumably there is very little satisfaction in sucking on a metallic piece of plumbing.

Since Mark's dream reveals his unconscious view of the homosexual act as a joyless encounter, why is he still driven to homosexual acts? As we noted, Mark is not a man who accepts the homosexual mode. He is struggling against it because it deprives him of other gratifications he needs. Further, he feels degraded and victimized by the character of the homosexuals he seeks out. Certainly, the dream tells us he is in conflict.

Or perhaps the dream is an occasion to tell someone else (an analyst, authority figure, lover, friend) that he is resisting his homosexuality. In fact, there is in his life at this moment an important operating element. Mark is having a love affair with a woman. With the dream appearing at this juncture, he is able to say to her (if he chooses to tell her the dream) that his homosexual life is unbearably degrading; that as a result of his "weakness" he lives in a frightening charnel house; that sucking on a penis is for him as gratifying as sucking on a faucet; and, he is a victim, a Jew preyed upon by Gentiles. Therefore, he is to be pitied, treated sympathetically, borne with while he goes through a difficult period of transition.

Each dream is a story, and the dreamer is the author. Every element of the dream is created to serve the needs of the dreamer. The curious twists that dreams may take are limitless. For example, there is reason to believe that people will manufacture dreams to satisfy the demands of others. Thus, a patient in analysis may dream just the kind of dreams he thinks the analyst wants to hear. This makes him a responsive patient and gains him the all-important approval of the analyst. With Mark, we are dealing with a complex and informed person. His fertile mind may well have created this dream for the purpose of communicating his plight to the woman whose love and understanding he needs. With such a dream, Mark might be striving to preserve his continuing homosexual compulsion by emphasizing to her its painful and degrading character, as well as his struggle against it. If he can enlist her pity and support, his pain and guilt over the homosexuality are reduced and he can continue the pattern.

So, we find that a dream may not only serve to represent an inner conflict and reveal underlying feelings, it may also serve the dreamer's need to defend his present behavior and conceal the truth from the dreamer and from others. But, when understood, this too becomes an important part of the truth. As Mark recognizes this, he then is able to realize that he has not yet achieved enough depth of understanding of his homosexuality to eliminate it.

From a short dream, a fragment really, we have been able to explore Mark's conflicts about homosexuality, his efforts to resolve important personal problems, as well as his resistance to changing them, and we have caught a glimpse of his feelings about the larger world of Jew and Gentile. This dream is a marvel of compression, yielding a great deal of pertinent information through a few well-chosen symbols. But Mark is also able to churn out richer, more varied and elaborate dream stories.

Sex, Spears and Symbiosis

On November 6, 1973, Marcus Foster, the superintendant of schools of Oakland, California, and his assistant, Robert Blackburn, were walking to their cars after a meeting of the Board of Education. Without prior warning of any kind, they were shot down by a fusillade of cyanide-tipped bullets and shotgun pellets. In this fashion did the snake of the Symbionese Liberation Army (SLA) first raise its seven heads.

In the spring and summer following, the world was treated to an extraordinary drama that played itself out day after day in the press and, especially, on television. Patty Hearst, the attractive twenty-year-old granddaughter of William Randolph Hearst, was kidnapped by members of the SLA. These people were a tiny terrorist group who appeared to combine and sum up some of the angriest social conflicts of our time.

The small group led the FBI and other police a long-running chase until the afternoon in south Los Angeles when the police assembled and destroyed six of them who had holed up in a small house on the fringes of the black ghetto. Never before had the worldwide television audience been treated to such a show: a live massacre in progress.

Compared to the handful of Crucifixion witnesses at Golgotha, we had, with the benefit of the supercool advanced electronic communications media, hundreds of millions of fans who turned off *Kojak, Cannon* and all the other imitation slaughter shows offered by TV in favor of the real thing.

In addition to the rare public aspects of this story, there was the intensely provocative personal saga of the "poor little rich girl," Patty Hearst, who publicly condemned her own parents as "Fascist pigs," who threw in her lot with a group of radicals, blacks, lesbians and violent men who had victimized her—to the extent of wielding a machine gun during a bank hold-up and firing such a weapon on the occasion of another robbery. Certainly, there was speculation in the minds of many about the nature of the relations of this girl with any or all of the members of the gang. Subsequently, it was established that she did have sexual relations with one of the men, Willie Wolfe.

Whatever may be the truth about Patty Hearst's character, emotional problems, family relations, social convictions, it is possible that this story is the stuff of which myths are made. It has everything: the kidnapped Helen of Troy; Electra conspiring against her father; Jesus and Barabbas; Romeo and Juliet; Robin Hood. Is it possible that this story will enter the collective unconscious as enduringly as these earlier myths?

Such sensational current events impinge on all of us and frequently appear in our dreams. But, alone with ourselves in sleep, we each turn the raw material of public fact into fabrications to suit our individual needs. Depending on these needs, we may dream that Donald DeFreeze (the chief black figure in the SLA) is either a frightening monster or a liberating hero; that two girl members who openly acknowledge their love relationship are debased perverts or, on the other hand, splendid specimens of the women of the future who deal with sex, politics and poetry in the freest and most creative terms. Is Willie Wolfe a weak and depraved white boy who has fallen under the sway of a degenerate criminal band, or is he a fine, strong, independent youngster who chose to die for his beliefs rather than live without protest in a corrupt world? And Patty Hearst? We all dream. What does one man make of it?

Mark, who is trying to cope with his homosexual behavior, had the following dream:

> I am with my own younger brother when Patty Hearst enters the room with *her* brother. They come in with guns and take me and my brother captive. People in another room don't know or don't care that this is happening. My young brother tries to escape from the room by climbing out a window but Patty stops him by sticking a spear into his lower back. My brother, the victim of this attack, removes the spear and is furious with the girl. Now, Patty's brother reenters the scene. He resembles a "middle-American" image of me. I fear that something awful is about to occur and I am very angry with myself for remaining passive. Then, I find myself in bed with Patty, and she and I are engaged in sexual intercourse. I am performing very competently but I feel that my penis is too small and, as a result, I will not be able to generate the total abandon and devotion that Willie Wolfe inspires in her.

For Mark, Patty Hearst perfectly symbolizes his ambivalence toward women. She is young, pretty, desirable. She is the helpless victim, first of her rich reactionary family, then of her brutal captors. She is in this sense weak, desirable, not threatening—and therefore, safe to make love to. On the other hand, she has become a member of a dangerous armed band of terrorists; she has thrown in with blacks, sexual deviants and common criminals. In Mark's dream, the girl is a gun-toting, spear-throwing creature. She is available for sexual experience but she wants a man with an outsize penis, a man like Willie Wolfe who is "masculine" enough to give up his life in a fiery inferno for a cause he espoused. Mark feels inadequate to satisfy such a woman. In life, this is what women represent to him: tough, aggressive, unreasonably demanding and intimidating, people who scorn you, people it is best to avoid. But, because he is trying to overcome his homosexuality, he makes an effort to relate to the part of the Patty Hearst image which is the victim, the weak and dependent girl we all imagined in the early days of the saga.

The dream of imperfect sex with Patty Hearst, who is a full-fledged SLA member, reaffirms his anxiety that he cannot fulfill the role of the male in our society (sexually or otherwise). Fearing failure, he chooses to play the female role in sex (i.e., coupling with a man instead of a woman). In the dream, he further reinforces his pattern by seeing himself as Patty's brother; he becomes the same flesh and blood as Patty; he creates a powerful identification with her. And, this tricky game of identifying with women is what he does in life. He is saying that it is better to be a girl because then no one can depreciate him as an inadequate man.

The identification with Patty Hearst in the dream has other levels of significance. We have seen that Mark, like the rest of us, has problems that go beyond the narrowly sexual. He feels, for instance, that he is a member of an oppressed minority. In the dream, he has sexual intercourse with the daughter of a rich and powerful WASP family. For the sleeping mind, this can easily be the equivalent of marrying the girl. The result of such a union would be to gain the love, power and protection of the family and, particularly, of the father, thus fulfilling another of Mark's needs. In still a different sense, the dream represents Mark's mating with a legendary figure, one who for good or ill has become mythic and outsized; coupling with such a "goddess" might well bestow fame and immortality.

There are other elements in this complex dream which reveal further areas of Mark's problems. The appearance of his younger brother undoubtedly signals an aspect of sibling rivalry which Mark could profitably explore. The image of Patty Hearst with a spear, sticking the brother in the "lower back," is portraying her with a dandy phallus and, again, indicates Mark's ambivalence about just what the girl represents: is she primarily a male or a female figure? The fact that Mark becomes a "Middle American" brother to Patty Hearst is, again, an expression of his recurrent anxiety about Jewishness in a hostile Gentile world. There is the telltale sentence, almost lost in the narrative flow: "People in another room don't know or don't care that this is happening." While Mark and his brother are being captured by the SLA terrorists, the rest of the world doesn't give a damn. Mark's feeling of isolation and alienation is clearly spelled out.

Every dream, then, is a reflection of the dreamer's most elemental needs. We will stop at nothing in our dreams. We seek only to serve our own needs, and we wish to be answerable to no one. Whether we deal in war and famine on a global scale, death and misery of the most intimate kind, the latest ball game, an encounter with the family pet or mythology in the making, we turn this raw material into meaningful patterns which, properly understood, tell us again and again about our sex lives, our interpersonal relations and our interaction with the world around us.

Homosexual dreams do not only occur to homosexuals. Characteristically, a man on the threshold of marriage may have such a dream which may be nervously interpreted by the dreamer as a lack of confidence in his masculinity; such a dream may be very theatening but, in all likelihood, it has little to do with the man's sexual identity. Marriage in our society is fraught with anxiety-provoking aspects, and the tired old jokes about hog-tying a man to the altar are not without foundation. The groom with cold feet may have a homosexual dream—not because he doesn't love the girl—not because he has reason to question his male identity—but because he is anxious about assuming a lifelong financial and emotional commitment; he is fearful of trading his "freedom" for an open-end contract. In these circumstances, the homosexual dream represents a fantasy alternative . . . an excuse, if you will, to flee from this burdensome compact. During sleep, when common sense and rational judgment are suspended, such fantasies may emerge to serve their defensive ends.

A woman with no homosexual tendencies dreams of having a penis and copulating vigorously with another woman. She may be expressing her protest against being assigned a passive and submissive role by the culture—or by a husband with whom she has a normal sexual relationship.

But beyond this, homosexual dreams must be accepted as a normal function of our minds because we all have both heterosexual and homosexual impulses. How could it be otherwise when we are raised by mothers whom we love and hate and by fathers whom we love and fear; when we learn during the years of growth (whether we are girls or boys) that we must emulate both our parents but also compete with them; when through all the years of sharply observant childhood we are forced to watch the interplay of masculine and feminine roles and assess the advantages and disadvantages of each? How can we not be ambivalent about our sexual identity? And *why* should we not be ambivalent? Why should such a premium be placed on absolute maleness and absolute femaleness?

We know that other cultures have accepted homosexual practice with considerable equanimity, cultures as far removed in time as the Greek and Roman, as far removed in sophistication as the Plains Indians of North America. But in our culture, at least until very recently, the occurrence of homosexual impulses has been seen as a fearful sentence to lifelong ostracism. The reaction, naturally enough, to such an impulse, whether in dreaming or waking, is very defensive. Defense is an aspect of the art of warfare and can be conducted either actively or passively. Passive defense may be represented by the thick-walled castle that isolated one's party from attacking forces. An individual who is fearful of his unacceptable social impulses (such as homosexuality) also builds a wall to hide behind. He shrinks into himself, becomes smaller; he shuns outside contacts, becomes narrower. His act of defending himself reduces him in every dimension, stunts his opportunities for contact and growth. The man who fears his feminine impulses and hides behind a defensive wall cuts himself off from developing the very maleness he so much desires. He cannot grow into a full male personality so long as he is hiding anxiously inside his moat. To paraphrase a bit of folk wisom: Be wary of what you fear, you're likely to get it.

But the arts of warfare developed beyond the castle defense and the fortified line when it was discovered that armies and people tended to decay behind their false sense of security, to become even easier prey for the attackers. A theory of dynamic defense evolved. Patton "defended" us by moving into battle with tank columns. Psychologically, we now turn from the strong silent man to the overly aggressive male who is defending himself from his disturbing dreams of homosexual encounter. Again, it is a self-defeating mechanism. The vast energy expended on proving one's maleness to oneself and the world exhausts one's available resources. We all know the excessively assertive male who isn't really that much of a man. It's important for all of us to understand the arithmetic involved. None of us has unlimited supplies of energy. If we try to defend ourselves like a Panzer division, aggressively denying all signs of femininity, we are going to exhaust the very energy we need to develop the truly male aspect of our personalities.

Of course, everything we say about the man and his feminine aspect applies to the woman and her maleness.

If homosexuals are accepted in our culture without repugnance or opprobrium, then all men can be freed of their defensiveness over their normal feminine vectors and freed to develop their male aspect more fully.

Whether you are a man or a woman, accept your homosexual dreams as a healthy ingredient of your total personality. Then, remembering that each of us is the product of a specific culture with a specific set of attitudes toward homosexuality, check out how you feel about your femininity (if you're a man); your masculinity (if you're a woman); how you feel about all the other men, women and children in your interpersonal constellation; and how you perceive various items on the national and international scene.

Homosexual dreams will regularly reflect a part of the dreamer's involvement with the men, women and children who are important in his life. Furthermore, a homosexual dream may well say something about the dreamer's perception of broader social issues. For instance, we have seen how Mark's sexual dreaming deals with his concerns about Jew and Gentile, his feelings that a cultivated man is degraded in his contact with Midnight Cowboys and his complex and contradictory perceptions of the emergence of political terrorism in the United States as exemplified by the SLA.

Others in their homosexual dreams may discover that, beneath the surface, they are dealing with different social issues of particular interest to them as diverse as a garbage strike in New York City, drilling for oil in the Santa Barbara Channel or the political drift in the subcontinent of India.

Unconscious Homosexuality

---❧∞❧---

So full of artless jealousy is guilt
It spills itself in fear of being spilt.
· HAMLET ·

TOM

The Fear of Male Identity I

I am lying in bed with a guy. He is a fellow I know from the YMCA. The guy is huge and powerfully built. We are lying there just like a married couple watching television in bed. Then, the man starts to make advances to me but he is being very gentle and tentative about it. I push him away and tell him that I really do not want sex with him at all. Actually, I am feeling tender toward him but I don't feel any sexual urge.

· 47 ·

Tom awoke feeling very uncomfortable, even angry. A dream like this he didn't need. He is very unfulfilled in his personal and sexual life and he is not succeeding in his career in a way that is commensurate with his genuine talent and superior education. So, this dream strikes him as insult added to injury. A man lies down for a night's rest after a difficult and frustrating day only to have a dream that evokes guilt, shame and doubt as to whether he is a man or a gay.

Reflecting on the dream, Tom recalled quickly enough that he had recently seen a fellow at the Y, a real muscleman, tough, no suggestion of tenderness. This made the portrayal of the specimen in the dream a real absurdity. But there is another man at the office where Tom works who is Tom's age, a friend and a bisexual. This man is tender, compassionate, attractive in his dealings with both men and women. Thinking about the men in his life inevitably leads Tom around to thinking of his father, who had long seemed to be cruel, manipulative and sarcastic. But recently, Tom visited his father in the distant city where he lives and the father had behaved uncharacteristically. He was ill and, for the first time, seemed kind and considerate. Later, Tom learned things which suggested that his father's unexpected warmth was an act, a fake, designed to elicit protection from Tom because his father was fearful about having a fatal illness. One more example of the old man's manipulative behavior. In fact, it turned out that the father was not as desperately ill as he had feared and he did subsequently recover.

Tom's father had a serious physical deformity and had always exercised zealously to compensate for it. As a result, his physique had always been and still is striking, like the strongman at the Y. Also, the father and the man at the Y are alike in that neither appears to be kind or tender. From his associations to the dream, there can be no doubt that Tom is wrestling with some problems that involve both his father and physically attractive males. Two elements stand out forcefully: first the portrayal of the man in the dream as sensitive and gentle; second, the clear homosexual wish (despite the thin disclaimer of no sexual urge at the end). Thus, we find in the dream an ambivalent wish: on the one hand a desire for the father to be genuinely kind and loving, on the other hand an unconscious wish to be sexually ravished by a powerful, sadistic man.

Acknowledging the first wish was disheartening since Tom was tired of feeling like a little boy who hoped Dad would be nice to him; but admitting the second wish was absolutely dismal. Still, Tom must face up to his feminine wishes and come to understand how such wishes play a role in his sad chronicle of relations with women. Tom had been married briefly to a very disturbed woman. In fact, such women were the only ones he could become involved with on a sustained and serious basis. He could care for and protect such women until finally his own starved feeling would cause him to break it up. Why this need to "care for and protect" a wife or lover? In Tom's case, this is a fiercely felt need to express the feminine side of his personality and play a mothering role in an intimate relationship.

Tom's specific sexual pattern for years has been one of promiscuity which he finds distasteful but unavoidable. Many women attract him and they, in turn, are drawn to him. The first time out, the sex is great but afterwards it's all down hill. By the third or fourth time they make love, Tom is bored, revolted and impotent. Often, he finds something physically objectionable about the woman: the shape of her legs, a special genital odor, a birthmark or whatever. He thinks this connects in some way to his father's physical defect.

Tom is bright and open-minded; he has learned that all men have a degree of unconscious feminine identification. Finding this out about himself will not plunge him into an orgy of self-denigration. Some men have more unconscious feminine wishes than others; but, regardless of degree, this factor in all men (and their inability to cope with it) accounts for much of the undesirable behavior men encounter in their sex relations with women (impotence, flat or premature ejaculation, etc.) Along with all of his brothers in this problem area, Tom does not have to choose betweeen homosexuality on the one hand or troubled sex relations with women on the other. Though, like the rest of us, he will never achieve some imaginary ideal of perfect sex with women, he can learn to accept both sides of himself, stop battling the feminine fraction and use the energy thus released to strengthen his male identity.

DICK

The Fear of Male Identity II

> I go into the bathroom to take a leak. I notice how large my cock is. Then, an attractive married woman comes in. I want to show her my cock and tell her she really needs me because of what a beauty I have. Now I realize in a hazy way that the woman is Sharon, my brother's wife.

Dick has familiar problems, feelings of guilt and sexual inadequacy. But the beginning of his dream shows him moving toward a healthier acceptance and enjoyment of his own male sexuality. Of course, the need to make his perfectly normal and satisfactory penis especially large in the dream betrays some lingering doubt about his maleness. The fact that his sexual drive is directed toward his sister-in-law shows us that the old incest bugaboo is behind his problems. His concern (comic in the dream) for the size of his penis occurs in the context of an incestuous urge. To be sure, it is his sister-in-law, not his mother; but the unconscious is saying in dreams like this, "No matter how you slice it, it's still incest." The dream reveals to Dick that so long as he carries around his guilt feelings for early incestuous desires, he will be troubled by some degree of uncertainty about his potency. Classically, a boy with a strong incestuous urge for his mother will, to an extent, recoil from his masculine drive and lapse into an unconsciously feminine attitude.

HARRY

The Fear of Male Identity III

> I see cunts, more than one I think. It's like a film with multiple exposures . . . lots of cunts moving around me and long female legs. I can go down on all these cunts at once and down on all these legs, bury myself in them, get lost in them. I am very excited. Now, they all seem to belong to one girl, Jane L., who married my best friend. The anatomy gets all confused.

Harry is a brilliant government economist and the author of some important work in his field. He has a most promising career ahead of him, but, like so many, he feels that he has never really been able to tap his own rich resources. These problems of underachievement (at least in his own mind) are related to his sexual problems.

The night before the dream, he had learned from his wife that his fifteen-year-old daughter had had sexual intercourse with a neighborhood boy whom Harry doesn't like. Also, he had learned only two nights earlier that his niece, about the same age as his daughter, had been seriously abused sexually by several boys. While he resents these youths, he cannot drum up any real rage against them. Harry has always felt guilty sexually; he has had little sexual experience except with his wife. He is chronically frustrated because when he becomes sexually aroused, he feels guilt, like a selfish schoolboy, not like a man who has a legitimate right to sexual fulfillment. Again, we encounter the problem of sexual identity. Because Harry is not sufficiently confident about his maleness, he must withhold the full uninhibited expression of his male sexual demands.

The news about his daughter and his niece has apparently stirred up an aggressive sexuality. These uninhibited boys engage in sex without guilt, even with cruelty (it seems to him), and Harry identifies with them because he permits himself to dream of a kind of direct and forceful sex (cunts and legs) with the wife of a dear friend. The dream, in the context of the real life events when it occurred, reveals the dreamer's wish for a freer, wilder, guiltless sexual pattern . . . like the boys who screwed his daughter and abused his niece. That he permits himself to dream and recall a dream so full of taboo (the wife of his close friend is like a sister) is certainly hopeful. While the background of his sexual problems is not explored here, it is enough for present purposes to realize that in his dream, Harry is struggling to free himself of guilt and is reacting even to a distressing sexual episode of his daughter's with a healthy sexually demanding dream of his own.

Harry feels, and we agree, that if he could unload his sexual guilt and inhibitions, he would become freer in the other areas of personal relations and career activity; he would make a qualitative leap forward in his ability to master the challenges of his life.

Impotence

---·•(∞)•·---

*Three fatal Sisters wait upon
each sin,
First Fear and Shame without,
then, Guilt within.*
· ROBERT HERRICK ·

ARNIE

A Bar Is No Bar

Arnie is an intelligent and scholarly man in his late thirties who teaches English in a large metropolitan high school and has become assistant to the department head. He genuinely likes his work and has plans for writing and publishing in the field of American literature. Arnie is married and has two young sons. He suffers much anxiety and depression and is intermittently impotent. In the school system, he is well regarded by his co-workers and by his superiors, although there is some feeling that he lacks the aggressiveness and firmness to function well on an administrative level. The department head is a self-assured man only about ten years older than Arnie but, because of his personality and position, he is regarded by Arnie as an intellectual and professional mentor. Arnie, who lost his own father in early childhood, is strongly inclined to regard his capable and amiable chief as a substitute father.

Arnie's other close relationship in the department is with a teacher, Yvonne, who is a strikingly good-looking woman only a year or two younger than Arnie. Yvonne is the acknowledged beauty of the faculty; she is liked and admired by all and lusted after by some. Although their friendship has been consistently platonic, Arnie has felt some stirring of desire for Yvonne but he is convinced that she is much too lovely, much too splendid ever to be sexually interested in him. Besides, on principle, he is faithful to his wife.

Now, however, Yvonne has been having serious emotional difficulties in her own life; she is angry and depressed and has become sexually blatant with Arnie, literally propositioning him. This has Arnie all churned up; he is excited, frightened, confused, tempted, guilty, angry with the temptress and clutching at a determination to be strong and withstand the sultry blast. In the midst of this mini-crisis, Arnie has the following dream:

> It's weird. I'm fucking Yvonne and at the same time we are sitting in a barroom having a drink and talking. First, I'm fucking her in her asshole, then I don't feel like that anymore so I turn her over and start doing it vaginally. While all this is going on, Yvonne is telling me that the department head wants to have an affair with her. I am surprised and I am trying to digest the significance of this as Yvonne goes on to say that the department head hasn't been able to get together with her because he considers his wife to be an obstacle and that he is planning to kill his wife! I am shocked, horrified that this man who has been the only

real father I've known would be hatching such a monstrous plot. I also sense that I am caught up in a sinister extension of his scheme; that, somehow, he planned this whole sexual encounter between Yvonne and me and that I am really doing with Yvonne what he wants to do. In a sense, I am doing it for him, doing it in his place. I am, in effect, being used by him to fuck Yvonne. I feel awful about this. It gets even worse when I sense that someone is glaring at me from the darkness at the end of the bar. I stare down the bar and finally realize that it's my wife's father who has been watching me all along! I don't recall how I felt at that point but it probably scared me because I awakened drenched with perspiration.

Though Arnie is aware that he has been troubled and conflicted by the new explicit sexual atmosphere between himself and Yvonne, it is something he has been able, on a conscious level, to put aside. The dream reveals how deep and intense is his fear of the possible sex encounter. In life, one form of this fear is a great dread that the department head may discover Arnie's secret passion, rip off Arnie's insignia, drum him out of the corps (out of the department, the school system, out of the chief's regard and affection). In plain words, Arnie feels that his passion for Yvonne is dangerous, even criminal and, if discovered, may result in severe punishment and loss. How does he handle these feelings in the dream? He makes the department head into the real culprit, the real seducer. Sure, Arnie is making love to the girl but the chief is the one who engineered the assignation; the chief is the one who is really enjoying it. This *reversal*, frequently encountered in dreams, puts the onus on the very person whom the dreamer fears—and effectively blocks any punishment and retribution. Clearly the chief can't attack Arnie for doing what the chief himself wants to do and even arranged for Arnie to do.

Evidently, this particular trick of reversal worked so well in the dream that Arnie carried it still further. He imputes to the chief a criminal scheme to murder his own wife when, in fact, it is Arnie who has become very impatient and resentful of his wife. It is Arnie's wife who is an obstacle to his having an affair with Yvonne; further, he feels that his wife has become increasingly selfish and infantile, refusing to assume any normal responsibilities around the house as wife or mother and Arnie often thinks these days that he would like to "kill" the relationship, divorce his wife; but he could never do this because of his love and concern for his children. Orphaned at an early age himself, he feels this inflicted serious damage, and he will not repeat this with his children. So that there can be no doubt about the real wife-killer in the dream, Arnie has planted a lollapalooza of a clue: he has placed his wife's father at the end of the bar, glaring down at him accusingly. Even in the dream, try as he may to unload all the guilt on to the chief (a father figure), he can't get away with it; there is his own father-in-law watching his vile behavior with Yvonne and, somehow, apprehending the whole nefarious scheme.

So, one point about Arnie's sexual difficulty, his impotence, that comes out in the dream is that though he is attracted to women, he feels murderous hostile urges toward them. He literally feels like killing his wife. This rage and its potential consequences terrifies Arnie, disarms him. It is with him whenever and wherever he is relating to women, especially during sexual intercourse. If his penis remains erect during intercourse, it is not the firm bridge of love, it is rather a lethal instrument of vengeance. Better to keep it small, soft and sheathed.

Further reflection on the dream develops a second meaning. It relates to the triangle of himself, Yvonne and the department head. Arnie has known and accepted Yvonne's "favorite child" position in the office family. It was okay so long as the chief loved him, too. With fondness, he would sometimes speculate about whether the chief and Yvonne were attracted to each other sexually. But when his own sexual interest in Yvonne became strongly aroused, he lapsed into a terrified dream where

the powerful male, the father figure, became the real ma-
nipulator, the dangerous killer. His sexual urges caused
him to feel, entirely without any foundation in fact, that he
was in competition with the older and stronger man, that
he was stealing a woman away from the other man, the
daddy, the boss; this made him feel criminal, fearful,
weak. Accordingly, a second basis for his impotence, as
disclosed by the dream, is his fear of sexual rivalry with
more powerful men.

Still a third point emerges which sheds light on Arnie's
problem of impotence: Arnie recalls that a couple of years
ago he dreamed of having anal intercourse with Yvonne.
This memory connects with how be began sex anally in
this dream, *then turned her over* (reversal) and proceeded
vaginally. A rather clear instance of reversal—from rear to
front. We have already seen a couple of instances of reversal in this dream (it is not Arnie but the boss who is really
screwing Yvonne; and it is not Arnie but the boss who
wants to kill his wife); since the mechanism of reversal
seems to be working overtime, what other kind of reversal
should we look for? We recall that the sex act in the dream
is essentially triangular involving Arnie, Yvonne and the
department head. Also, the department head appears to
be the one who arranged and manipulated it all and is the
one who seems to be enjoying it the most so it is not really
Arnie who is doing the fucking, it is the chief. And who is
the chief fucking? Yvonne, to be sure. And how is he fucking her to start? Anally. Is it possible that this portion of
the dream represents another reversal, that it is not
Yvonne but Arnie who is being buggered by the department head? Wouldn't that help to explain the dream concept that it is really the department head who is enjoying
this sexual encounter most? Is it possible that Arnie's
dream is saying, "I want the boss to make love to me, to
penetrate my body, to enter me through my anus?"

Arnie has not been homosexual; he isn't sexually attracted to men. On the other hand, there was some puber-
tal homosexual experimentation. Furthermore, through-

out his life, he has hungered for a father. He has even had thoughts that if an older man would accept him as a son and show him how to be a man, he would, in gratitude, do anything, even distasteful sexual things, for him.

Generally, impotence can be related to three significant issues and all three certainly appear to converge in this most revealing dream: violent hostility toward women; sexual rivalry with more powerful men; and a submissive sexual wish for a father figure. This constellation of problems has for years kept Arnie less than potent sexually, has colored all his personal relations with men and women and has resulted in a characteristic impotence in his relation to work, career and life in general.

II

SEXUAL
DREAMS
and
INTERPERSONAL
PROBLEMS

From Here
to Identity

---⟨∞⟩---

There are few chaste women
who are not tired of their trade.
· LA ROCHEFOUCAULD ·

PHYLLIS

A series of remarkable dreams dreamed by a remarkable woman follows. These dreams constitute a modern woman's odyssey, her struggle to reach her sexual, her existential Ithaca. The adventures, temptations and triumphs are abundant and varied; they deal directly or indirectly with the universe of sexual conflicts, identity conflicts and value conflicts in which all modern women live.

Basically, this is a love story.

Babylon Revisited

> It is early morning, sunrise, and I am inside somewhere
> with my lover. Then I am walking back to my own home
> with my older daughter. But I have unfinished business
> with my lover. I go back. I find myself in a horrid slum.
> The men are leering and threatening bums; the women are
> sleazy streetwalkers. With difficulty, I make my way past
> these vile creatures and struggle to my lover's room
> through legions of attacking rats. What transpires in the
> room is not clear. Then, I leave again through all the filth
> and vermin.

The dreamer is Phyllis, an attractive woman in her thirties. She has two young daughters and she has been divorced for about one year. She is having her first sexual
relationship since her separation. But the man is remote,
cold and enigmatic. Phyllis herself is frightened, feels sexually inadequate and undesirable. She feels exploited by
this ungiving man, but she is being quiet about her anger.

Phyllis has a twin sister, Helen. She grew up in a home
where intellectual achievement and social responsibility
were expected of the children. This was no hypocritical
demand, since Phyllis's mother and father were both dedi-
cated physicians truly devoted to public service. The Puri-
tan ambience of their New England home penetrated
every fiber of Phyllis and her sister who grew up with social values very similar to those of their parents. It was
thoroughly understood by the growing girls that as children they should study hard, thus preparing themselves
for an adult life of creative work for the good of mankind.
In this almost missionary setting, sex was of no apparent
importance. Although Phyllis knew her parents cared
deeply for each other, retrospectively she realizes that
they never showed any physical signs of their mutual regard and affection.

By adolescence, an apparent division of labor became
evident in the growing girls: Helen became the sexy one,
and Phyllis became the "brain." In a sense there is nothing
wrong with such specialization. But in another sense,

which Phyllis understood later, this development did show that she was becoming uneasy over the increasing inner urgency and pressure of her sexuality and was building intellectual defenses against it. (Helen's counterpart problems will not be dwelled on.)

So Phyllis was by young adulthood living in accord with her own highly developed set of social and personal values, compliantly and dependently pleasing her parents through her life-style, and *very importantly but unwittingly* warding off her frightening sexuality. By now she was convinced that she was sexually insufficient and could not achieve the sexual feasts of other women (like her sister) and would have to settle for crumbs.

Why is this a love story? Phyllis, as a child, loved her father deeply. This love being natural and naïve did not know conventional limits. So it was strongly sexual. For whatever reason, her father could not accept the sexual elements in Phyllis's love, although he received and returned her love in other areas. (A normal father will unconsciously appreciate the feminine sexuality of his growing daughter, even when she is very young. Such acceptance by the father will be unconsciously communicated to the daughter and this is a crucial factor in her acceptance of her sexuality. Of course, in a healthy father-daughter relationship, the father will not be overtly sexual or significantly seductive.) From an early time, Phyllis sensed that there was a powerful but ill-defined remoteness in her father's involvement. Only later did she appreciate it as sexual repudiation.

Phyllis, nevertheless, married early. However, the marriage was conceived, grew and eventually died under a sustained condition of sexual rejection by her husband. Unconsciously, Phyllis had selected a husband who would continue her father's denial of her sexuality. Although children, mortgages and guilt are powerful girders and mortar to maintain the marital edifice, a marriage without real sexual love is a shaky marriage. Phyllis regressed, found herself unable to accomplish even simple household tasks or be very responsive sexually. One purpose of these incapacities was to shore up the marriage. Phyllis's overdependence on her husband enabled him to maintain his view of Phyllis as an inadequate woman who required his competence. He resented the burden, but this arrangement enabled the husband to hide his own inadequacies from himself by feeling superior and seeing inadequacies only in his wife.

The tension and discontent for Phyllis mounted. While she experienced herself as a deficient person in her marriage, she demonstrated imaginative and creative leadership in feminist, political and community activities. For a year or two prior to separation from her husband, she began to realize that the marriage could not work, and she began to resume her responsibilities in running the household. They separated by mutual consent.

The above dream occurred at the time of her first sexual experience after the divorce and is clearly pertinent to her augmented struggle to achieve full sexuality. Although in this affair Phyllis did not have orgasm, she did enjoy a modest degree of sexual pleasure. The special satisfaction was the feeling of being wanted physically by a man.

She knows that in the dream the scene of her lover among streetwalkers represents his devaluing her as a person; also it expresses her tendency in personal and social relations to see men as devaluing and degrading women. The sex, itself, is incompletely portrayed in the dream (what transpires in the room is not clear), symbolizing the incompleteness of her sexual response. Still, Phyllis is defining herself as a sexual woman in the dream, however much she distorts the image.

Phyllis does have some tendency to think: if I am sexual, then I am being a dirty animal and not the fine human being my parents want me to be. However, she quickly sees this as a transparent rationalization—an attempt to shift her attention from her real inner conflict over *her* sexuality to a spurious value conflict.

So the streetwalkers seem to be a complex symbol of Phyllis's conflicts over her sexuality and her perception of

society's confusing messages to women about sexuality
(be sexual, be asexual, cherish your body, sell your body,
etc.). There is a Dostoyevsky-like aspect to the dream: the
paradox of morality through degradation, an aspect that is
congruent with Phyllis's sensitive intelligence.

Thais

Only four or five nights later, evidently emboldened by
her first excursion into prostitution, Phyllis had another
dream:

> I am with a girl friend. There is a police car nearby. I enter a
> building which is a very elegant brothel. I accompany a
> man into a room (but I don't know what my role is sup-
> posed to be). My children interrupt, starting to call me.
> Next, I am outside on a street corner, waiting for a bus. No
> bus appears. I cannot get home.

Again Phyllis dreams of prostitution, but now she is no
longer among debased pathetic streetwalkers; she has
achieved a certain elegance, albeit a trifle sleazy. But
courtesans are not just perfume, epigrams and political in-
trigue. The job does require some dirty, degrading work.
Again a portrayal of social reality and Phyllis's inner sexual conflict. The police car reminds Phyllis that Anti-Sex is
vigilant. She is still very guilty. She is confused and un-
clear in the dream about why she goes into the room with
the man, and in this way she strives to reinforce her sexual
innocence.

Phyllis has moved from the Augean stables of the first
dream to the splendor and squalor of Alexandria. In either
location, however, she is still unable to find her lost lover,
the father by whom she still feels sexually rejected.

Vested Virgin

> I am sharing a house with another girl friend. A young
> man I know is visiting among a group of others. When the

other visitors depart, I come out to bid them good-bye. But I am unclothed above the waist; my breasts are bare. I am in a hurry. Now my roommate and the young man and I all drive to a theatre where my roommate becomes involved in a religious ritual. Meanwhile, the young man and I wait outside in the car. I regretfully assume that the young man is interested in my religious girl friend, but he tells me that for the first time he is sexually attracted to me!

Phyllis is clearly encouraged. In this dream, she is asserting her sexual equality with other women. The prostitution theme has vanished. A man prefers Phyllis to another woman. A desirable man may well prefer Phyllis to her "sexy" sister, the woman with whom she is sharing a house, and the same may be true in regard to all her other sisters in humanity. More basically, considering the genesis of her problems, there is a renewal of hope that her father can acknowledge her sexuality. This is the root source of sexual confidence. For if the parents cannot affirm a child's sexuality, how can the child ever possibly achieve this dimension of health?

Striking changes are going on in Phyllis's life. She is much less depressed. She is enjoying her children, her job, her friends, her social activities. She feels more confident with men, less frightened of rejection by them. She sees men as people like herself, not as different and menacing. She is clinging less to her parents, and she is enjoying them more. Whereas in the past she was in dread of angering her father, she is now amused, almost tenderly, when he loses his temper with her. Obviously she is moving closer to a great personal victory, but also there will be increasing dangers. As she becomes bolder in her acceptance and enjoyment of her sexuality, her deeply rooted guilt will not sit idly by. It will take all necessary measures to restore its dominance. This is the inevitable dialectic of each person's life. As Norman Mailer writes so perceptively in *The Armies of the Night*: "For guilt was the existential edge of sex. Without guilt, sex was meaningless. One advanced into sex against one's sense of guilt, and each time guilt was successfully defied, one had learned a little more about the contractual relation of one's own existence to the unheard thunder of the deep—each time guilt herded one back with its authority, some primitive awe—hence some creative clue to the rages of the deep—was left to brood about."

This time guilt does herd Phyllis back. In fact, she is hurled unexpectedly and roughly onto the rocky shores of the Island of Lesbos.

Lesbian Dream

> I am with two Lesbian friends who take me to a gay women's party. In the dream, I decide I want no more to do with men and I go to bed with one of the friends. I recall no details but I know it is the best sex I've ever had. Then, the friends introduce me to another woman, someone who is very attractive, with fine auburn hair. I like this woman and have sex with her, too. But it is vague.

For the moment, guilt prevails and, in her unconscious, Phyllis moves to the homosexual alternative.

Phyllis is somewhat puzzled by this dream. It reveals that she has unconscious homosexual trends; the two female sexual partners possibly reveal her sexual interest in the two women closest to her—her mother and sister. Most likely, she is frightened by success, and her increasing self-acceptance as a sexually competent woman threatens a full-scale eruption of her longings for her father (longings which are still far from acceptable to her or to him).

This situation conveniently brings to mind how in recent years a number of her woman friends have adopted a homosexual life and have recommended it highly as a way out of the eternal man-woman hassle. Phyllis has considered this alternative for herself at those times when she has felt most discouraged over finding a man to love. However practical (and impractical) this alternative lifestyle might be, it is not an alternative for Phyllis. She is sexually attracted to men—not women—except in an occasional dream.

As a humanist and a feminist, Phyllis does not regard her homosexual friends and acquaintances with fear, hostility or depreciating amusement. Nor does she idealize them. She questions everything. Although she does not agree that homosexuality can be a behavioral norm, she does know that the question of homosexuality has an importance for a number of feminist theoreticians because through the centuries women have been deprived of equal rights and have been valued largely for making and rearing children. This conjunction of social and sexual subjugation has caused some theorists to view homosexuality as the only logical sexual alternative for oppressed women. So Phyllis wonders if symbolically, this dream, which is a retreat from heterosexuality, may also be an expression of her increased confidence that she is becoming a full woman and an equal person. Thus renewed by reflection, Phyllis moves on in her search.

Finale—the Theme within a Dream

> I am in bed with one of my current men friends (one I am not sleeping with). We intend to make love but we are both so tired that we fall asleep instead. When we waken [she is still dreaming], we both feel marvelously refreshed. An extraordinary curtain is hanging down from above and separating us. It is gauzy, translucent and has an ancient Oriental pattern. I am fascinated by this filmy "screen" which separates me from the man. The man, however, is eager for me and has no interest in artistic embroidery. He brushes the curtain brusquely aside and takes me in his arms. We begin to make love. From his first touch, the whole experience is tremendous. This is the kind of perfect sexual linking of which I have always "dreamed" . . . wild, tender and complete.

Phyllis was moved deeply to have this dream and she recalled it with great pleasure and satisfaction. The dream was one of joy, lust, love and intense sexuality. In her waking life, Phyllis was becoming ever clearer about her conflict over her father and was now far past the midpoint of its resolution. She was particularly pleased by her comfortable versatility in her relations with men. As she became more accepting of her active and passive inclinations, she also became more accepting of these trends in men. She knew she was now ready for more sustained love and sex and, in almost miraculous manner, this soon began. She found a lover who, with her, fulfilled her wildest sexual dreams of days and nights intoxicated with sex—imaginative, intense, orgasmic. And all this in a relationship of friendship, mutuality and freedom. Phyllis does not know whether theirs will become a lasting relationship, but they value each other and it's great while it lasts.

As Phyllis was taking these huge strides toward her sexual identity, she began to observe with amusement a minor change in her behavior with men toward whom she has friendly feelings. She began enjoying "little things," courtly gestures: having a door opened, a car door closed for her, a protective arm around her in the rain or a brisk wind. This seemed to tie in with the very traditional symbolism in the dream of the man pushing aside the curtain and possessing her. Phyllis has become able to enjoy and accept herself, including her flaws and imperfections. And the dream suggests that as she becomes a more mature woman, she is also able to appreciate the complexities and difficulties in the traditional relationships of men and women. The classic submissiveness of women was not pure economic slavery. Like the curtain in the dream, it also had woven into it distorted patterns of love between men and women which have lasted through the centuries and cannot be simply eliminated by radical rhetoric.

Why can Phyllis now accept being cuddled, physically protected by a man? Perhaps she has discovered an eternal, immutable norm. Perhaps she has become more accepting of a flawed tradition. And perhaps she has discovered and accepted her girlish love for her father which persists in every woman.

Phyllis has had a very important journey. From a frightened, hurt, self-repudiating child, she has become a sexual woman. She has rediscovered the lost love. In a way, she has shown herself and her father that sublimated sexual love between father and daughter is as good as it is ancient.

Phyllis cannot foretell the future, but she looks ahead with hope and strength.

Extramarital Sex

*It is so far from natural
for a man and a woman to live in the state of marriage,
that we find all the motives which they have for remaining in that
connection,
and the restraints which civilized society imposes to prevent separation,
are hardly sufficient to keep them together.*
· SAMUEL JOHNSON ·

In married life, three is company and two none.
· OSCAR WILDE ·

NANCY

Licit, Illicit and Split

I am being shown a new house by a woman realtor. It is going smoothly until I notice a railroad track going right through the middle of the house. I tell the realtor that this makes the house unacceptable because it would be too noisy to sleep at night with trains rushing through the house. Now, I become aware that Hal, my lover, is with me and at the same time I notice that the backyard or rear patio ends in a dangerously steep precipice and I begin to feel fearful about someone in my family falling over the cliff. I cautiously approach the precipice and realize with relief that it was a false perception; actually, there is a gently descending meadow sloping down from the edge and covered with a beautifully tawny growth. Hal insistently proposes that we have sexual intercourse in front of the house, but I am afraid we will be discovered and I suggest we do it at the side of the house. We follow my suggestion and then I notice that Jim, my husband, is there—possibly with a woman.

Nancy has been married to Jim for almost ten years. There are children and, though there are frustrations and conflicts in the marriage, Nancy finds it difficult to contemplate breaking it up. However, secretly, Nancy is frustrated in the sexual relationship, though her husband thinks it's dandy for both of them. Recently, Nancy has become involved in an affair with Hal. This is a passionate and sexually satisfying relationship, but Nancy is convinced that Hal would be an impossible husband in every other way. She is conflicted about her dilemma day and night. Much of the time she feels virtually torn apart, unable to choose between the men, unable to relinquish either. So, as is often the case, the house in the dream represents herself, and it is she who is split into two parts just as the railroad splits the house apart.

It can be fascinating to play with some of the obvious symbolism in a dream. For example, the railroad track and the train are strongly sexual in connotation, so it appears that it is the sexual liaison which is threatening to break up the house Nancy has been living in so long—with Jim. The house, we have said, is Nancy herself. But dreams are much too rich and free to be inhibited by any narrow-minded limits of consistency. An object in a dream may stand for more than one idea. The house, here, is not only Nancy who is split in two, it is also the life she has built with Jim, a life into which Hal intrudes very insistently.

Behind the house, there appears to be a dangerously steep precipice which arouses Nancy's fear of someone falling (to destruction?). But this is a dream and wishes intervene: the precipice turns out to be a false perception. Instead, there is a beautiful gently sloped meadow. (She seems to be telling herself in the dream that perhaps there is no real danger; perhaps she can enjoy both Hal and Jim in the neighborhood of this house.) In reading the dream or listening to Nancy tell it, it is well to recall that it is Nancy who has "written" the entire script. Nothing happens in this dream unless Nancy arranges it. Hal has no free will of his own. He is, in the dream, entirely a puppet with Nancy pulling the strings and writing his dialogue. If Hal "insists on sexual intercourse right in front of the house," it is because Nancy wants him to insist on it. Why? Perhaps she wants Hal to say (in life): "To hell with this sneaking around; to hell with your marriage; I will assert my rights as a lover, my authority, manhood. I will tell the world, including your husband, that you and I are lovers." It appears from this that Nancy really wants to ring the bell on her marriage. This is further confirmed by what occurs next in the dream.

Nancy suggests the side of the house for her sexual encounter with Hal (keep it hidden). Another meaning of this is her wish for secret spicy sex, having a lover "on the side." But even there she finds Jim (you can't keep it hidden). And Jim is there, possibly with a woman. The woman could be Nancy herself, who belongs beside the house with Jim—not with Hal. Or it could be another woman who will replace Nancy in Jim's life if Nancy doesn't quit fooling around with Hal.

A dream with so much detail can be explored almost without end. With the help of Nancy's associations, such a dream could be used to reach back into her early feelings about sex, marriage, love, guilt, security, her role as a woman. What is significant here is that, while awake, Nancy appears able to handle the dual role she is playing, but the dream denies this. It reveals that she is not one of the people who can carry on like this blithely and indefinitely. She is deeply troubled; she is split, and she is

heading for worse emotional problems if she doesn't succeed in resolving the situation between herself and the
two men. There is, too, the strong suggestion that Nancy's
unconscious is far out in front of her and that she has decided to break with Jim, though she isn't yet aware of this.
(Subsequent to writing the above, Nancy did decide to
make the move forecast by her dream. She made her
choice and moved out of the marriage.)

As Nancy continued her thoughtful scrutiny of this
dream after her divorce, she discovered that beneath the
manifest sexual content, there was not only the complex
sexual substructure already discussed; there was another
complete set of meanings revealed and concealed by the
sexual symbolism. Simply put, Nancy recognized that her
relationships with both Jim and Hal lacked emotional va-
lidity and that the whole feeling of a split in her sexual at-
tachments and loyalty really expressed her split feelings
about her own identity as a human being. In addition to
the cleavages along the usual lines of feminine-masculine,
adult-child, motherhood-career and the like, another split
of an unusual nature was portrayed here in the form of the
sexual symbols.

This has to do with Nancy's long-standing conflict about
her social position. Nancy is a descendant of one of the
oldest and most distinguished families in America. She is
extremely wealthy. She proudly carries the family sur-
name, and she considers her children to be the future of
the dynasty. At the same time, she strives desperately to
be regarded by her friends and acquaintances as just a
regular, liberal, middle-American girl who checks the
newspapers for the weekly meat bargains at the supermarket. *Noblesse oblige*. Marie Antoinette and the milk-
maid—she strives to be both. She knows she must eventually choose parts of these two vastly different social roles
and fuse them into her specific and unique identity. The
house in her dream, which is split so dramatically by the
railroad line, suggests the "house divided," the conflict
over her class position as well as her related conflict over

her sexual situation. The directly sexual part of the dream, choosing between Hal and Jim as lovers, also stands for her conflict over which social role to build into her identity.

As she moves toward a solid, realistic, and satisfying definition of herself as a person, she must establish her social identity, and vice versa. Neither can succeed without the other. A miniature class war is raging within Nancy; the aristocrat versus the bourgeois. Parts of Jim and Hal represent her upper-class orientation and parts of Jim and Hal represent her middle-class self. Nancy's multiple splits prove no global theories, nor does their healing offer any grand design for living. But they do offer an interesting example of the direct, if complex, relationship between sexuality and social role and position. They demonstrate the many levels of meaning that may be encompassed within a single sexual dream.

Love and Hate:
Fathers and Sons

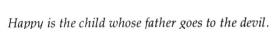

Happy is the child whose father goes to the devil.
· 16TH-CENTURY PROVERB ·

GEORGE

Sodomy

George, a man who is fifty years old, has the following dream:

> I am being sodomized by my father! It is all quite explicit but I have a strange *mélange* of feelings. I am horrified and excited; but also I am strangely indifferent.

George has always had a normal sex and family life, so this is not the dream of a practicing or latent homosexual.

A successful attorney, he grew up in prosperous and outwardly conventional circumstances in a medium-sized southern city. But he was the only child of a near-psychotic mother who fiercely overprotected him and created a close relationship with the boy which she denied her husband. There was from the beginning a heavy tension between father and son, a sense of rivalry for the mother, that was scarcely the boy's doing.

The mother died when George was thirteen. Thereafter, the relations between George and his father were scrupulously correct but lacking in warmth and demonstrativeness. At an early age, the boy left home for school, attended a distant university, earned his professional credentials and settled in a city on the Pacific Coast as if to place the maximum distance between himself and his father.

Then, a lifetime of constraint was shattered by this dream of violent and unnatural intimacy. The dream of sodomy was very disturbing to the adult, who wondered whether it might betray a latent homosexuality. We think not.

George grew up in terror of his father who, not so incidentally, was a meat-packer; this is not the same as a butcher, but the two may be easily confused. It is a heavy burden for a boy to live with the sense that his large, all-powerful butcher of a father is competing for the mother's attentions.

It is all too common for a mother to use a favored son as an "ideal male," not demanding sex, an example of a "good relationship" to counter the husband's normal marital desires and the normal tensions that arise between two adults in marriage. The mother sets up a rivalry with which neither the son nor the father can cope. The boy is terrified that the father will literally destroy him. Considering the buried but evident sexual nature of the rivalry and considering that the father is a "butcher," it is not unlikely that the boy's fear of destruction takes the form of a fear of castration. Remember: the boy did have sexual designs on his mother; he did enjoy being favored over the father. All his life, then, the son continues to feel guilty that he successfully wooed the mother away from the father and fears that the father will retaliate violently.

When the anticipated punishment arrives, it comes in the form of a dream. By dreaming of the father's violent assault that takes this particular form, the son is acting out his fears. It is a kind of pyschodrama. The dream episode, while violent and brutalizing, falls short of death and literal castration. In his dream, the son is offering a bargain to the injured father. "Take my body but don't kill me or cut off my balls." In submitting to sodomy, he is settling the score by offering a merely symbolic castration, playing the female role in the sex act with the father.

There are undoubtedly other elements. There always are. There is a likelihood that the son yearned for a closer relationship with his father from the beginning, especially after the mother's death. Left without that parental tie, he was also denied one with the hostile father. He must have felt doubly rejected. Thus, the dream may also be a bid for the father's affection and attention, an offer to replace the dead mother if only the father will be loving.

Does this last suggest that there may be, after all, some latent homosexuality in the dreamer? Sigmund Freud emphasized repeatedly that children have a polymorphous sexuality and have some sexual interest in both parents as well as in their brothers and sisters. Freud scandalized his Victorian colleagues with this completely amoral view of children's natural sexual appetites. Even now such a view of children is difficult for some people to accept.

Because homosexuality is an area of taboo for many people, homosexual dreams are a source of fear and embarrassment. But the homosexual dream is as likely to occur to the straight as to anyone. It is the unconscious trying to tell you something you should know, possibly about totally other areas of repressed, forbidden or even rewarding sex.

A highly analyzed friend who never had any problem in this area once remarked that early on he had encountered

·homosexual dreams with a certain dread. Maybe it was true, as his wife occasionally asserted, that he was a "fairy." But now, after additional and more fruitful analysis, he welcomes the encounter with a man in his dream and looks forward to discovering where it will lead. Instead of cutting the dream short, he permits it to play itself out.

In certain tribal cultures, like the Senoi of Malaysia, we are told the following occurs: a child dreams of falling, becomes frightened and wakes himself up. The father tells him: "You must relax and enjoy yourself when you fall in a dream. Falling is the quickest way to get in contact with the powers laid open to you through your dreams." Hopefully, more of us can learn to use our dreams so wisely.

George recalls an episode that occurred when he was five or six. The foreskin of his penis became so tight (phimosis) that he could not urinate and was in great pain. The doctor came to the house, evaluated the situation and decided that the condition had to be relieved at once. He placed the confused and frightened child on the kitchen table in the mother's presence; then, without further preliminaries, seized the swollen penis and roughly forced back the foreskin. What resulted was that the already exquisitely tender area was excruciatingly torn, spurting a fountain of blood and probably convincing the terrified child that everything had been cut off. The doctor's brutally direct treatment did, indeed, relieve the immediate condition but it caused another kind of trauma which has never entirely healed.

In the history of another individual, such an episode might have been a painful but passing event. In this instance, the bloody and threatening treatment of the penis reinforced a number of troubling factors: father was a butcher (meat-packer) who was already associated with a lot of violent bloodletting; father was jealous of the sexual overtones in the relationship of the son and mother; the anxiety about castration because of the mother-son-father triangle undoubtedly preexisted the episode reported; the doctor, an impressive male authority, could easily be confused in the mind of the child with his father. All this resulted in some inchoate but insistent conviction in George that he had been sexually mutilated. Subsequently, the death of the mother and the strained relations with the father did nothing to relieve the boy (later, the man) of these feelings.

Now, some forty years later, George has the following two dreams:

Cunnilingus
and *Punishment*

> I engage in very exciting sexual foreplay with my attractive twenty-five-year-old stepdaughter. Then, I go down on her. I waken suddenly.

After he goes back to sleep that same night, he dreams again.

> There are snakes in the grass. I am attempting to kill them. I kill one, decapitate it, really cream it!

Later, when fully awake and thinking of the dreams, especially the one about the daughter, George experiences considerable anxiety related to having such strong forbidden wishes toward his steppdaughter. You may well be of the opinion that it is entirely natural to want to kiss a pretty· twenty-five-year-old girl anywhere at all. Further, if she is a stepdaughter, it adds a delicious aura of guilt, i.e., she is certainly forbidden fruit but the act is not as absolutely rotten as in the case of a natural daughter. However that may be, society frowns on such practices. We are clearly far over into the area of taboo. George, despite his dream, is certainly not the kind who would ever indulge in such behavior. So he is disturbed and wonders what it all means.

At twenty-five, the girl has reached maturity and blossomed into a lovely young woman who uncannily reminds George of his mother, all the more because she has become a legal stenographer which had been his mother's work. As a boy, George had strong incestuous drives toward a mother who encouraged and stimulated such desires. When the mother died just as he was entering puberty, George felt forever deprived of any fulfillment in that area. But, now, in his full maturity, he has another dream of incest . . . but incest all the same. It appears that he is finally living out, in his dream, the original forbidden sex urge with his mother. This is what makes it so wildly exciting and threatening. The need for incestuous satisfaction, so long repressed and delayed, finally bursts out in this dream of sex with his stepdaughter.

Why cunnilingus? Why not the straight sex act? There appears to be a number of reasonable answers to this: Given a strong sexual urge toward the girl for whatever reason, George feels much safer performing cunnilingus than actually penetrating her with his penis. In a sense, this represents less of a sexual commitment. Incest is defined in the dictionary as "sexual intercourse between closely related people." Is cunnilingus sexual intercourse? Could a curbstone lawyer argue that it is something less and plead guilty to a crime of lesser degree? Is it possible that in this way he tries to protect himself from the punishment of castration he has so long feared for the very act of incest?

Further, it is significant that this girl first came to live with George as a stepdaughter when she was thirteen. She had just lost her father even as George, at the same age, had lost his mother. She was a tall, skinny girl, still sexually undifferentiated to outward appearances. She might almost have been a boy; she might almost have been the same boy he was at thirteen. The man felt an extremely strong sense of identification with the girl, this orphan, this thirteen-year-old child without a penis.

Now, in his dream, he is kissing and loving the penis-less sexual parts of this girl/boy with whom he so closely identifies. What is it like to have it all cut off by the father/doctor? Maybe it's not so bad. At least he can reassure the girl/boy (himself) that what's left is very desirable; indeed, wildly exciting. The "emasculation" has not left her/him without sex appeal.

W.hatever else the dream may mean, there is much that goes back to the relationship with the mother and the father, the episode with the doctor, the death of the mother and the propitiatory sodomy dream with the father. But unable to resolve all of this in the middle of the night, George goes back to sleep and dreams of decapitating a snake! He is compelled to carry out the dread sentence of execution and himself chops off the head of the eternally sinful and damnable snake. Note that he reports this dream with a certain zest. He not only kills the snake but goes on to say, "I decapitated it! I creamed it!" For one thing, he is balancing the moral accounts. He is paying for his just-experienced dream transgression with the stepdaughter by the relatively painless symbolic emasculation (chopping off the snake's head). On another level, he has been fearing and anticipating the castration for so long that it is a relief when it finally occurs. Sometimes the burden of guilt feelings is so heavy that one welcomes the punishment which relieves, at least temporarily, the sense of guilt.

Apart from his disturbing dreams, George had a serious, potentially dangerous problem on a reality level. Though successful in his career and financially comfortable, he had in recent years plunged into a series of financial ventures with a transparently unreliable promoter. Under normal circumstances, George was much too wise and experienced to be taken in by such a schemer. But he continued to plunge, sending good money after bad. He behaved like a compulsive gambler who, driven by insupportable feelings of guilt, must continue to throw the dice until he is cleaned out. Such a gambler wants to lose and usually continues to play until he does lose disastrously, thus punishing himself for his imagined transgressions. More than the advantages of the big bankroll and the house odds, this psychological factor is the secret weapon of Las Vegas.

George, though camouflaging his gambling as legitimate business ventures, was following the same pattern, attempting to pay for his enormous guilt toward his father, mother, wife, stepdaughter and anyone else you'd care to name.

This series of dreams can help George to understand the innocent origin of the guilt feelings he has carried with him for so long and so destructively. The repetition of the incest situation can help him go back to the original incest drive when he was a child and experience again the depth of feeling, so long repressed, which existed at that time. Out of this reliving can come an understanding that his original little boy sex drive was natural and universal; that the special circumstances created by the conditions of his parents' marriage exacerbated the seductive posture of the mother; this in turn aggravated the father's jealousy and menace; the mother's illness and death, coming when they did, multiplied all of the problems and, only incidentally, the situation with the doctor and the penis became a point around which much of his guilt and anxiety could crystallize. If George can relive and comprehend all this, he will at last understand that none of this was his doing; none of it, certainly, was his "fault" and there has been no reason through all these years for him to feel guilt or apprehension.

It would be fine if we could all say: "It's natural and healthy for a little boy to want to have sex with his mother. Who else can he possibly make it with? Who else loves the little stinker enough? It's nothing but a normal and universal impulse." Having gotten this far, it's possible to speculate on the next step and consider what would happen if we said, "It's natural to want to have sex with an attractive stepdaughter." The latter, of course, is quite a different matter; we are not discussing the natural original infantile drives of a small child and his parent; we are speaking of adult behavior. We are not saying that incest between consenting adults is advisable. But we do feel that it is a question that should be studied (if anyone is interested) in terms of its social implications, more than in terms of sin and guilt.

In any event, the practice of incest between adults is not

an important issue in our world. What is important is the crippling sense of guilt we all carry because of our infantile incestuous desires. Is it really necessary to beat such feelings into every child, or can we conceive a society that might flourish without this?

In discussing the implications of George's dreams and of his impulsive behavior, one seems to define him in terms of incest, sodomy and castration trauma. Perhaps, he begins to sound like a real sick one, not "normal" like the rest of us. This is not true. He is a highly successful professional man; he is respected by his colleagues; he has achieved an enviable position among his peers; he has a marriage that works better than most and he has decent warm relations with his several children and stepchildren. He functions. He is no more sick or neurotic than the "norm" of our society. That's why his story is important. If he has problems, we all have problems, and mostly we have the same or similar problems even if our dreams are not precisely the same. If he needs help, we all need help. If he can get help, we all can get help.

Sexual Immaturity

⸻⟨∞⟩⸺

(to music)
I want a girl just like the girl
that married dear old dad.
Song, 1911
Music by HARRY VON TILZER
Words by WILL DILLON

MICHAEL

Some Thoughts on Masturbation

It is not many years since masturbation was termed "self-abuse" in polite society and children who "played with themselves" were threatened with everything from syphilis to hellfire. In crueler times, children were physically maimed for the sin of Onan. In our enlightened era, one may witness the following scene: Mother and Father are entertaining guests at a sit-down dinner. Jimmy, age six or seven, is standing in the dining room doorway in his pajamas just as the wild rice is being spooned up with the mushroom sauce. Jimmy is pulling thoughtfully and unabashedly at his pecker. The parents continue their hosting with frozen smiles, unable to yell at the kid for fear of traumatizing him and forever crippling his chances for good genital sex. The guests try not to notice.

Elsewhere in this book, we have noted the universal presence of guilt in relation to sex and that it seems impossible to have meaningful sexual feelings without guilt. No one knows where the most basic sources of guilt feelings are located. We do know that guilt arises from the deepest levels of the human soul, and we know that shame, embarrassment, humiliation and self-depreciation are close relatives of guilt. So human desire interacts with human guilt, and out of this interaction human meanings are created. It is as though desire says, "Go ahead," guilt says, "Stop, think of the dangers." Who can say that action is better than reflection? Obviously both are necessary. So guilt is not only a powerful and painful emotion, it plays a crucial and constructive part in the human experience.

We know that a sense of guilt and shame restricts the amount and variety of sexual activities of human beings. So we often assume that sexual restrictions are limited to humans; we further assume that these restrictions are imposed solely by society—especially Judeo-Christian society—and finally we are tempted to assume that if these restrictions are lifted, sexual freedom will prevail and happiness will surely follow. However, sexual restrictions are not limited to humans. Most warm-blooded animals, including some very primitive ones, develop strict incest taboos—not in the young, but in those animals that reach the age of sexual maturity. This fact strongly indicates that restrictions on certain human sexual behavior (incest, masturbation, adult-child sex, etc.) may not be due solely to social and cultural factors.

Throughout the centuries, the struggle in individuals between their sexuality and their guilt has naturally been absorbed into the social and political institutions of mankind. An unfortunate and all too frequent phenomenon has been the perversion of guilt into an antihumanist instrument for destructive overcontrol of individuals and groups. The exaggeration of the sense of sin is an example of this distortion by society.

Nothing induced such a pervasive sense of sin as the old-time religious attitude toward masturbation. It was a subject that involved every child and every family almost all the time. What other major sin could be indulged in so easily, so covertly and leave so little evidence? What other sin, committed by a child, could fly so boldly in the face of God's injunction? Or lend itself so readily to deception and the bearing of false witness? The cruel abuse of sexual guilt in man developed to the extreme in the Victorian era. Our institutions and values are still recovering from the malady. Sexual guilt became affiliated with the industrialism and colonialism of the nineteenth century. This affiliation helped "adjust" people to unjust social conditions, to ensure that men and women would accept established social conventions and authority because otherwise they would feel unclean and unworthy. And sexual guilt became an ideal tool for regimentation rather than reasonable control of social behavior. Unfortunately, no one really gained from this surplus sexual repression. Not even the lords and ladies enjoyed fulfilling sexual intimacy. Husbands had their mistresses because love for a woman had to be split: it was spiritual toward one's wife and carnal toward one's mistress. And what of the wives? We need only recall the well-worn story of the upper-class English girl in 1892 who goes to her mother for sexual advice on the eve of her marriage. Mother offers this simple wisdom: "Darling, just close your eyes, grit your teeth and think of the Empire!" Everyone was damaged by sexual guilt run wild.

Certainly it is very early in life that our little man has his hand slapped away from the genitalia, so he begins to learn "right from wrong," "self-control," guilt (anticipation of punishment)—in short, learns to carry on as an acceptable member of a structured society. Of course, masturbation is not the only form of sexuality proscribed: no incest, no homosexuality, no peeping, no sex at all until after marriage. These injunctions are effectively distilled through countless generations of human experience, not necessarily to be obeyed. They are like the twenty-five-mile-per-hour speed limits posted in most of our cities. No one respects them but, because of them, we all know that we are lawbreakers, that we are helpless to defend ourselves from the police if caught for *anything*. We plead guilty. We have no defense. We must be punished.

So the transgression of excessive and abnormal sexual taboos—the external authorities and the internal authorities we carry within our minds—disarms us in our struggle with authority. As very young children, we are utterly dependent on our parents for love and life. They fertilize the soil of infantile guilt. Under this pressure we tend to accept our state of sin. We grow into stifled compliance or blind rebellion. Parents, then teachers, entrap us into obedience to police, rabbis, priests, coaches, sergeants, doctors, lawyers, Indian chiefs, bankers, politicians, labor leaders.

Dreams disclose our basic personality patterns. In order to understand them better, we must see how a small matter such as the disapproval of the infant playing with his genitals can contribute to the structure of repression and crippling that occurs. Sexual taboos are a primary means of shaping the new human being into a form acceptable to society. It is instructive to observe how frequently, when there is a significant change in the power structure, there is a new wave of sexual repression, of puritanism; this appears to occur whether it is the rise of a merchant class in post-feudal Europe, the conquest of Saigon by the Viet Cong or the accession to power of Qadaffi in Libya.

Dreams, our most intimate and uninhibited form of self-expression, have the power to reveal our sexual confusion to us. Dreams can help us retrace the tortured road we took from infancy which led us to the cross of sexual impotence, guilt and abuse. Dreams can show us, despite censorship, what forbidden sexual games we would like to play with mother, father, sister, brother, teacher, cop, doctor, husband, wife. Dreams can help us to understand how our distorted sexual attitudes have been transmuted into inhibited social attitudes. And, since we are all human beings with a unique ability to understand ourselves, reject ourselves, remake ourselves, we may certainly learn something from dreams that will help us to change our behavior and our outlook which otherwise condemn us to repeat in each generation the repressions of a past that may no longer be appropriate to the present circumstances of life.

Even when dreams appear to have no relation to sexuality, you will find if you dig enough that they do. For dreams always deal with personal relations and attitudes and our attitudes and patterns are, from the beginning, related to sexuality.

What about the mother and father who were sitting with guests at the dinner table trying to ignore little Jimmy? Hooray for them! They are trying. They're moving in the right direction. But since their own guilt about masturbation exists and will undoubtedly be sensed by the child, and since repressive attitudes about sex are subtle, pervasive and ubiquitous, it is too much to hope that within the period of a single generation they will be able to free themselves and their offspring of a heritage that goes back into the dim mists of man's beginnings. But they *are* making a start, and it appears that our own generation of young adults already shows a healthy questioning of the warped aspects of sexual and social conventions, thanks to the efforts of better-oriented parents.

What If Mother Knew?

Michael, at age thirty, dreams:
I am looking at *Playboy* magazine and I am "beating off." When I come, it just dribbles out very unsatisfactorily. I feel very guilty and have the awful thought: "What if my mother knew of this?"

Michael is a professional man. His years of growing up had been troubled by the fact that his father suffered a chronic and potentially fatal illness. Because of this, the boy had developed an exceptionally close relationship with his mother who had been the one to share his intense interest in athletics, had taken him to ball games, had, in short, performed those rites usually reserved for the father-son relationship. The boy had unconsciously developed a resentment of the father for "failing" him. During adolescence, Michael also developed severe obsessive-compulsive rituals such as counting and washing. One obsessive issue was that if he failed to perform the ritual, his father would die. As an adult, he complains of a diminished sex drive and lack of intense satisfaction during his frequent sexual encounters.

The masturbation dream gives us a clue that Michael is trying to cope with adult sexual problems in an infantile way; probably, too, that he is struggling with his problems and trying to grow into more satisfying and appropriate sexual behavior. But, apart from the question of sexual behavior, it is worth remarking that we have evidence that the past remains very much alive in us. An intelligent, highly sophisticated adult dreams anxiously of his parents' disapproval over his naughtiness in masturbation. This is not the child dreaming, nor is it the man remembering the child. It is the man reflecting attitudes that operate here and now, very actively in his unconscious and appear nakedly only in his dreams. By recalling such a dream, by understanding it, Michael may begin to ask why he still operates on the childish level of needing parental approval. And he may ask whether he carries such an attitude, not only into sex, but into all of his relationships, seeking approval from teachers, lovers, peers—approval for not being a wicked and sinful little boy.

Oedipus Wrecks

Michael has other dreams which shed light on his problems.

I am starting to have intercourse with a young woman friend, who draws away and objects that this would amount to incest. Then, in the dream, I go to an appointment with my father but, on arriving, learn that my father has died. I suffer extreme anguish over this news, a great sense of loss and guilt. The feelings in the dream are so intense that I wake up.

The sex act with a "woman friend" who complains that this would "amount to incest" is a thinly disguised wish for sexual intercourse with the mother. But with the taboo of incest being raised, the sex act is aborted. Even in the dream, censorship is strongly at work. Then, Michael moves on to an appointment with his father (the agent for punishing him should he, in fact, perform an act of incest) and finds that the father is dead. The convenient death might, within the logic of a dream, remove the obstacle to incest and therefore represent a wish. But the wish for the father's death is fraught with terror and the feeling of guilt so unbearable that the dreamer wakens to escape the scene. This dream, then, is an exceptionally naked example of the Oedipal conflict; an attempted sex act with the mother and a "murder" of the father.

But this dream has failed. It has not masked Michael's emotional pain well enough and he has wakened with acute feelings of guilt and loss. Freud said that the function of the dream was to permit the dreamer to go on sleeping and, thus, continue to wrestle peacefully with his unconscious problems. On the following night, therefore, Michael tackled his problems more cunningly, eliminating all overt sexual content.

Spectator Sport

I dream that I am attending a·closed-circuit television presentation of a major sports event (boxing, soccer or baseball). However, in my section of the auditorium, the screen is concealed from my view by a curtain or wall partition so that I am not able to see the screen at all. I am only able to hear the sounds of the event. Toward the end, even the sound dies out. I am angry. I feel cheated. As the dream continues, I go to my father and tell him that I may file a claim of fraud against the promoters. My father anticipates that the promoters will rebut my charges by alleging that I should have known what I was buying. In the dream, my father is passively reassuring.

In this instance, the manifest (apparent) content of the dream is based on the circumstances that Michael, only a few days before, had attended a closed-circuit showing of an international soccer event. At the real event, the visual portion failed during the final twelve minutes of the big game. The irate spectators almost rioted. Superficially, then, Michael was working out his hostility toward the promoters of the sports event (authority figures) and obtaining some passive but welcome reassurance from his father (authority figure) that, at least in principle, he was justified in harboring feelings of resentment. Recalling the dream and analyzing it on this level might help Michael recognize and dissipate the stored-up irritation growing out of the fouled-up event.

On a deeper level, though, we find other meanings. The scene is forcefully reminiscent of the little boy who manages to hear what is going on behind the curtain, the partition, the wall—but is not permitted to witness the "main event." This dream of the so-called primal scene, i.e., sexual intercourse between the parents as conceived by the child, reveals the little boy who resents the normal sexuality of his parents, who feels excluded and is jealous of the father who is in bed with the mother. The dream also tips us off about Michael's attitude about the imagined event going on behind the curtain or wall. He views it as an aggressive event: boxing (box); soccer (sock her); baseball (base; balling). The dreamer (spectator in the auditorium) feels cheated and injured, feels wrongfully excluded; he wants to enter a claim for damages but, after talking it over with his father, he feels that he will get little satisfaction if he complains to the management. He will be told that he was attending this show at his own risk; no one forced him to be present. In the dream, when Michael conveys his dissatisfaction to his father, the old man is "passively reassuring" as though he is saying, "It's okay, sonny, nothing to get excited about. Business as usual."

This dream deals with much the same material as the dream of the night before, i.e., Michael's sexual interest in his mother and his feelings of hostility and competition with his father in that particular arena. But the form it takes is a substantial retreat from the naked incest and parricide of the earlier dream. This one does not waken Michael nor does he, on wakening in the morning, experience any strong emotion. His "sinful" attitudes toward both mother and father are sufficiently disguised so that he is unlikely, without outside help, to raise the meaning into his consciousness and be able to recognize the infantile feelings he still harbors. But, though less blatant than the first dream, the same elements are there: the intense interest in the parents' hidden games, the feeling of being excluded and the deprecation of the father.

How do we justify dragging in this sexual interpretation of a dream which, on the face of it, is merely a replay of something that actually happened to the dreamer in recent days? There are several answers to this: First, when Michael thinks about the dream, he dredges up feelings and associations that lead right back to his childhood and the situation we describe as the "primal scene"; second, the pattern of the scene is classic and occurs again and again, the curtain or wall or closed door shutting the dreamer off from the all-consuming event he wishes to witness; third, the principle which always prevails in dream interpretation, that a dream must be examined on two levels, the level of the manifest content (the actual closed-circuit television presentation) and the level of the latent content (the underlying and deeply rooted patterns of feelings which are developed out of early childhood experiences or fantasies and often accessible only through dreams).

In case we are still skeptical about the connection of Michael's current sexual difficulties and his attitude toward his parents, particularly his mother, let's look at some more of his dreams.

I Never Left Home

> I am in bed with Dolores, a Nisei girl I have known for some time. We are both naked on top of the covers. The bed is in the middle of an enormous room—or it is more like a room without any walls. It is like an island in the middle of a dry sea (Japan?). The colors are remarkable. I've never tried any of the psychedelic drugs but I've read that they produce extraordinary color hallucinations; or it's like the corny light shows they used to have with the rock music performances a few years back. The colors are flashing all around us. It's not alarming. It's exotic and pleasing. And there we are on the bed. I'm delighted by her full breasts and fascinated by the color of her nipples. She starts to shiver uncontrollably as if I have already entered her, and she moans words in a strange language. I wonder if it is Japanese, although I remember even in my dream that Dolores doesn't speak anything but English. The low clicking sounds that come out with each breath are wildly stimulating. I am now unable to contain my excitement and I am just moving on top of her, when my mother walks up to the bed and we have to stop everything, pretend nothing is going on. I feel very frustrated.

Michael, as we said, suffers from impaired ejaculation and feels sexually frustrated, although he leads an active enough heterosexual life. Dolores, the pretty Nisei girl, is an old friend who in her quiet way is probably sexually interested in Michael. But despite the fact that he is attracted to her, he feels inexplicably compelled to avoid a sexual relationship with this girl.

Certainly it is no accident that his sex dream is interrupted by his mother. All of his sex problems are related to his tough, controlling, seductive mother. As with so many in our culture, Michael has been aroused and seduced from an early age and, simultaneously, conditioned to hate himself for his incestuous inclinations. Sex, all sex, becomes forbidden or tainted by taboo. He dares not let go and really enjoy his ejaculation with a girl because that would be like yielding to his early sexual urges toward his mother. So, his sexual encounters, though desired and sought after, are always damaged by a lively sense of guilt.

The dream of Dolores suggests that he would like to move far away from the usual fields of sexual battle to an exotic relationship where the colors are more vivid, the sounds and forms unfamiliar. Perhaps, there, he could escape from his sexual constraints, find more fulfillment, true release. But, no, his dream tells him that his mother will pursue him even to the Far East to rob him of his pleasure. He is in an impossible bind: if he wanders to the Orient, he must feel guilt for abandoning his mother; if he stays home, he must feel guilt about his nasty incestuous wishes for her.

Further, since Dolores is a real girl, not a figment of a dream, it is worth recalling that Michael is unable to bring off a sexual relationship with her though, apparently, both of them desire it. Is it because he fears his mother's disapproval? Would she frown on a relationship with a girl of a different race? Isn't it obvious that even at his mature age and, despite a varied sex life, he still feels compelled to consult his mother's atittude toward that sex life, even as he worried in his dream about masturbation and how his mother would react if she knew?

The appearance of the mother is not at all unusual in sex dreams but this is an exceptionally clear example of the continuing influence of the mother on sexual behavior, an influence that goes on and on throughout an individual's lifetime.

Michael's sexual problems, as is so frequently the case, go to the question of his masculine identity. Having been raised in exceptionally close relation to his mother, he tends to identify with her and her female characteristics. Also, as we noted, he has rejected his chronically ill father who failed to create a good functional male pattern for Michael to imitate. His sexual dissatisfaction reflects a pattern of guilt and self-denial growing out of his forbidden wishes for his mother and his frightening wishes for his father, but it goes beyond this; it goes to the question of his sexual identity. Considering the factors that operated between Michael and his parents, does he see himself principally in the male or female sex role? He dreams:

Playing Doctor

> I am going to my doctor for another of many consultations about my sexual difficulty. While I am starting the session, the doctor hands me a bill for $2900. I think, "Jesus, I only have $2400." I have to go through the stress of borrowing all that money from Dad; he'll give me the money but he'll lecture me on being too extravagant and irresponsible. It was my understanding that at this session with the doctor, we are just supposed to talk but, instead, there is this examining table and either he is supposed to get up on it or he wants me to get up on it because he finds it rather uncomfortable. Suddenly, right in front of me is a face which looks like a combination of my doctor, a fifty-year-old man—and Sally, my girl friend. I wonder what it would be like to kiss him/her. The face is young, pretty and feminine-looking, but it's really a man . . . ugh! Pfui! Then, I am just about to screw Sally. I'm really turned on and I vaguely appreciate the presence of ruffled panties.

Michael had a course in sex therapy in which a surrogate taught him tricks and techniques for relaxing and developing more staying power. The sex therapy resulted in some improvement, but not enough; so Michael continues to see his doctor in more conventional analytic therapy. Michael is, by now, capable of ruthless honesty about himself. He wastes no time, when thinking about this dream, on preliminary rationalizations such as dwelling on the heterosexual aspects in a defensive way. This, clearly, was a homosexual dream. But the homo- and heterosexual parts were closely connected; the fusion of male and female in the other person's face was the dream's way of pointing out the connection.

As he thought about the dream, Michael recalled that on the day before he had been having a sexual fantasy about a girl at work and that during the fantasy he began to wish he were a woman; a woman can have more fun in sex, writhing and screaming, relaxing, letting go, no worries about getting hard or staying hard or keeping control. A woman can just lie there and let it all happen to her; whether it works or not is the man's responsibility; a man has to stay cool, maintain control, or he'll come too soon and louse it all up. He has to work at it, worry about it, put himself on the line—anything but simply enjoy it. This was Michael's spontaneous feeling; it was his fantasy and, of course, most women would dispute its objective reality. Michael is honest enough and sophisticated enough to admit readily that, in fact, women must participate actively in sex, work their way up to climax, help the man, respond sensitively, be a sex partner, not a passive object. Michael's tendency to fantasize this way in connection with the bisexual nature of the dream gave him a good deal of solid evidence about his suppressed feminine wishes. He was now beginning to accept that he must give these wishes freer rein on the assumption that if the wishes were no longer so rigorously repressed, he could enjoy his predominant masculinity more.

The formula may be expressed as follows: in order to repress his frighteningly feminine side, he has to divert much of his masculine "energy" to this purpose; this actually depletes his store of masculinity. When he can relax and accept a certain degree of femininity, he will therefore have more masculinity and be freer to enjoy it.

Michael is an exceptional athlete; he has achieved success in his work and he is actively committed to volunteer work in a major consumer-oriented group. He takes his social responsibilities seriously and has much to offer. But at every level of his life, he darts in and darts out or hangs back like a shy little boy. He lacks the confidence to go all the way in any project or to display the kind of leadership his abilities warrant. Always, he feels that he must present a cool, controlled facade. If he is loud and asserts his views with force, he fears he will be seen as an hysterical woman, not as a strong man.

His anxiety about his feminine side, his fear of being exposed as less than a hundred percent male, damages not only his sex life but manifests itself in every area of his life. Again, sexual problems are never restricted to the sexual arena; they are a paradigm of our total behavior.

To some degree all men are crippled by this struggle to deny the feminine component they harbor (and how could they not; didn't they all have mothers?). The more *macho* the man, the more we may suspect that he is covering up. Perhaps only when women are no longer considered the weaker sex will this pattern begin to disappear. In this sense (and it's an important sense), full equality for women may free men as much as women. Meanwhile, *vive la différence* should be accepted not only to celebrate in the literal sense that male and female parts—electrical, plumbing and sexual—fit together so neatly and satisfyingly, but in the broader sense that we are all richer for having and accepting the yin and the yang that happily coexist in all of us.

If Michael seems to be an exceptionally troubled man, we are doing him and you a disservice. We find him more like the majority of men of his class in our culture than unlike them. It's only that he has worked on his problems, brought them closer to the surface, where he can study them, dream about them, work on them so that we can all benefit from examining what is typical, what is commonplace, what has meaning for the rest of us. Sexual difficulties are certainly not uncommon; the problems involving the achievement of sexual identity are virtually universal in the area of our purview; and so, too, in various disguises, is the problem of self-assertion which Michael experiences. Certainly, the individual factors of his background are unique for Michael and for each of us, but the emotional issues resulting from these factors are familiar to the rest of us as may be apparent from a discussion of his next dream:

Voodoo Equals Doo-doo

> I dream again that I am attending a sports event. This time it is a basketball game. Just before the game is due to start, I have a strong urge to move my bowels; so, annoyed with myself and loathe to miss the entrance of the players, I go to the men's room.
>
> There, I find that there is only a single toilet which is being used by a small boy whose parents are with him and making a big production of it. I am eager to get back to the auditorium and infuriated by the delay. I am forced, however, to observe that the child's parents are engaged in a complex ritual with the toilet paper. It is some kind of voodoo, a curse. Finally, when impatient and most uncomfortable, I do get to the toilet, I find that it is stuffed with filthy toilet paper. Though I am furious and revolted by the mess, I am caught up by now in the matter of the voodoo curse.

When Michael wakens, he recalls having watched a television medical show that involved voodoo that very same evening before falling asleep. This helps to explain some of the manifest content of the dream. As related earlier, Michael had serious problems during his years of growing up. One form that his problems took was in the area of anality. Thus, during the night, if either of his parents used the toilet, he was revolted; he felt soiled. This was especially true if defecation was involved. He would engage in an extensive cleansing ritual, turning his pillow a fixed number of times and touching himself magically in various places according to a rigid schedule.

To this day, although he has had considerable sexual experience with any number of women, he can *never* recall seeing or touching a woman's anus in the course of sexual activity. There is an absolute exclusion of anything relating to the anus in his conscious sexual life. Further, dark-haired women put him off sexually because they remind him of his mother and the possibility of being exposed to her anal odors.

But it is the combination of anality and voodoo that comes through so strongly and interestingly in this dream. Voodoo equals doo-doo equals shit. Voodoo is also an ethnic form of black magic and associated with black people. This brings out another of Michael's problems. As a boy, he had extremely close ties with a black family that did domestic work in his home. The black woman was a surrogate mother. To this day, he feels that these people are virtually blood relatives. For a while, as a young man, he was strongly attracted sexually to black women. Later, this attraction turned into active aversion. Along with this he developed a generalized hostility to black people and their ways. The garment of society is so thoroughly saturated with racism that it will not be eliminated quickly or easily. It will take a lot of Tide, Cheer and Woolite to launder out our sick and corrupt attitudes toward the colored people of our own country and the world. For a long time yet, even the best-intentioned people will be dreaming of black bogeymen. There are decent people who, in their waking life, are convinced that they are free of racial prejudice but who in their dreams will discover strong remnants of this sickness. There are conscious and sophisticated people who understand the difficulty of rooting out such prejudice, who admit there are remaining traces, who are determined to fight it; yet even they will be surprised by the revelations of their dreams. They will resent profoundly waking from a dream of being raped by a black man with an enormous and threatening penis. They will blame themselves for harboring such dark thoughts. But they, too, are victims; they, too, have seen our country go to war against dark-skinned "gooks" and "slopes" in Asia on the easy assumption of superiority over colored people, an assumption nourished by generations of racism at home.

It helps to understand the extent and pervasiveness of our prejudice when we see Michael, a man who grew up in a northern metropolis, whose father is a respected jurist who would fiercely deny social prejudice, whose mother is also a sophisticated professional woman, whose family took a black family into their home and treated the blacks (or thought they treated them) like blood relatives—this man, now an adult, dreams of black magic (voodoo) and excrement in a single linked image. This man who in his waking life cannot resolve his attitudes toward black women, veers between feelings that they are the only truly exciting sexual partners and turning away from them with disgust.

There is yet another element in the last dream that is at least as significant as the clue it gives us about racial feelings: the subject of magic—any magic whether black or white, superstition or religion. It is instructive to find this same contemporary and "liberated" man responding in his dreams to the horror of magic. But we all do. If the taint of racism is almost ineradicably pervasive, the stain of superstition is even more basic, going back beyond Eden, beyond Olympus or even *The Golden Bough*; beyond all history and anthropology. Who were the first men to believe in "god" or animistic spirits or in a pantheon of immortals? What was the first religion? When, as man rose to his hind legs, began to use his forepaws as hands, formed intelligible sounds with his tongue, teeth and throat, when did he first say god or devil or magic, spirit or power of darkness? Whenever that occurred, whatever the meaning of the impulse to explain the world in supernatural terms, to seek comfort and security through propitiation of the unknown, it is still with us.

However rational an individual, however agnostic, atheistic or sophisticated in his religious beliefs, you may be certain he is also to some degree superstitious. He may seek out black cats and force them to run across his path; he may go out of his way to walk under ladders, break mirrors, ignore wood to knock on and sneer at the concept of luck, but you will find him responding to the chill of a

good horror film, trying to beat the odds at Las Vegas or
sneaking a look at the astrology forecast in the morning
paper. You will find that in countless ways there are hints
of his vestigial belief in an eye in the sky that watches,
judges, rewards, punishes. How could it be otherwise in a
world where so many influences bend us to the belief in
some form of the supernatural?

If, like so many today, you believe yourself free of religious conviction yet find yourself dreaming of magic, of
angels, of ghostly spirits, of heaven and hell, you are in
the same company as the rest of us. If you are completely
enlightened but dream you are being chased by a devil,
and the devil is a great deal like a black man you've met,
then you are winning the daily (nightly) double; you are
demonstrating that dreams do not lie about your unconscious, and that your unconscious is formed by the same
everyday influences that have worked on all of us for
countless generations.

Even if our parents were determined to eradicate all
traces of supernatural fear and conviction, such tendencies
remained in their marginal and unconscious attitudes. We
encounter these relics more nakedly in grandparents,
friends and neighbors, on television, in films, books, nur-
sery rhymes, at school, on the team, in the national pledge
of allegiance, in the songs and poems that are some of our
most precious heritage.

If you are offended by evidence of superstition in yourself; if your dreams betray even more of it than you imagined, remember that it grew with you through all the days
of your life like the grain of the wood in a plank. It cannot
be erased or planed away. It goes all the way through.

Michael grew up in an atmosphere where there was no
overt bigotry, with parents who despised superstition and
elevated rationality. He has a better than average start on
understanding the roots of his problems. He can readily
accept the existence of dark unwanted corners in his unconscious; he does not bitterly resist the implications of his
dreams; thus, he can move toward insight into the origins

and etiology of his problems. This is the longest step toward cure.

Cure? Do we mean that he will overcome entirely every vestige of his attitudes toward blacks, toward excrement, toward magic . . . and sexual guilt? No. We mean that he will be able to behave reasonably toward blacks and understand his own limitations when the impulse is to do otherwise. He will not be obsessive about anal problems, and he will be able to enjoy sex more fully even if he chooses not to explore his partner's anus; he will accept that there is a large component of the feminine in his makeup and not permit that to damage the male part of him, which he enjoys. He will increasingly understand and be amused by his reaction to superstition and relegate that to the back. burner along with remnants of sexual guilt. He may suffer occasionally from an unpleasant dream in any of these areas, but this will only help him to understand himself a little better and keep him from backsliding.

The Land Governed by a Child

By education most have been misled;
So they believe, because they so were bred.
The priest continues what the nurse began,
And thus the child imposes on the man.

· DRYDEN ·

CHRISTINE

Soiled by Mother

I am with my mother and I am naked below the waist. There is brown watery feces over my crotch. I angrily say to my mother, "Don't dump your shit on me!"

Spoiled by Father

I am in a room with my mother and a graying, well-dressed man. He has 007 tricks in a shoulder-strapped handbag. Out of this bag, he takes a sharp-pointed vial which contains a small amount of whitish fluid. He injects this into my left upper arm. I am alarmed. I try to get the fluid out, fearing it will cause instant death like cyanide or curare.

Christine is in her mid-thirties, divorced and with several children. She is severely depressed by the very real problems of her life and has begun to realize that she has lost her psychological balance. She recognizes the barrenness of her relationships; she has no close female friends and keeps her several sisters at arm's length. She has men friends and frequent love affairs but these invariably founder when her enormous dependency needs collide with the man's.

Now a hypersensitive woman, Christine grew up with parents who were highly creative and busy people. They had little time or patience for their offspring. Christine was a shy, hypochondriacal, quietly angry child. She felt that her mother could not abide the biological by-products of infancy and early childhood such as soiled diapers, spit and vomit. She recalls that such matters were handled by strict, impersonal hired women. As in her dream, she feels that her mother left her dirty and smelly in her own excretions. She feels that she was rejected by this neurotic mother who was never able to accept the human body with its excreting and sexual functions. Christine, as evidenced in the dream, regards her own sexual organ as dirty, and she clearly places the blame for this on her mother.

In the succeeding dream, a romantic older man, probably the father in light disguise, appears. The father was a police detective, hence the resourceful CIA type in the dream. But, in the dream, the man, though attractive, is a lethal figure whose needle-penis contains "a small amount of whitish fluid" (semen? poison!) which renders the hapless female victim paralyzed or worse.

So, in her dreams, Christine finds herself trapped between an immature resentful mother who would like to wash her hands of the whole mess of child rearing—and a seductive father. This is a wicked combination guaranteed to create problems for the child and for the adult who emerges from such a childhood.

The dream symbols are painfully unambiguous: the feces on the woman's sex organ; the blaming of the mother in the dream; the older man injecting a semenlike fluid into the woman. There can be little doubt, whatever the "objective" truth about the family relationships during Christine's childhood, that this is how she experienced it, this is how she feels it, how it continues to live and operate inside her.

The fact that Christine can dream about all this and relate it with so little dissembling tells us that she is prepared to examine the traumas of her childhood and try to cope with them. She will have to go beyond recognizing her hostility to her mother, recalling her mother's distaste and rejection, entering the touchy area of incestuous feelings for her father (and by her father) but at least she is not blocking all of this and denying herself access to the many repressed feelings described in the dream.

There are other symbols in the dream that may help to shed light on Christine's problems. For example, there is the distinctly feminine shoulder-strap bag carried by the father figure. Here, Christine may be telling herself in her dream what she dares not think while awake—that her father had a significant feminine identification that interfered with his assumption of an effective male paternal role. Also, one may speculate about why the fluid was injected into her left upper arm rather than, say, her right leg, her buttocks or squarely into her vagina.

Of course, a dream is rarely completely transparent. The dream does not say openly that this is an incestuous act. The father is not specifically identified. The injection comes from a vial, not a penis. It goes into the arm, not into the sex organ. The white fluid is presented as a poison like cyanide or curare, not semen. The unconscious plays these games because the dreamer's censors are at work demanding a degree of deceit and camouflage. The dreamer resists knowing the naked truth. Like most of us when awake, we do not have the courage to face all the truth about ourselves, our problems, our limitations. As in the TV commercial, we prefer to listen to a friend who, mercifully, doesn't say, "Your breath is bad" but, instead, will tell us delicately about the fine new mouthwash he has discovered.

Beyond the fact that the dreamer (even in the superprivacy of his own dream theatre) wants to disguise the truth from himself, there is something else at work: the unconscious, while it has formidable powers because it is the repository of all the experiences of a lifetime and tends to feed back those experiences in various forms, is not some kind of infallible deity who sits back, observes all and understands all. The unconscious has the morality and perception of a great warehouse into which all of one's experience has been crammed helter-skelter. Whatever comes back out of that warehouse door most certainly went in through that door at some time (and it is important to respect this fact); but by the time anything comes out it may be mixed up with a dozen other experiences, faded beyond recognition, crusted over with mold, even broken into bits by the disorderly storage process. That's why it sometimes takes a specialist to fit together the fragments of a dream; or, to mix the metaphor, why it requires painstaking effort like that of a skilled archeologist reconstructing a whole civilization from shards of bone and pottery. Because of the nature of the process, we cannot expect dreams yielded up by the unconscious to be simple, clear and unambiguous.

Again, there is the poetic compression of dreams, the creative economy where the dream uses the same symbol to express more than a single concept. Thus, a man's handbag in this dream suggests a James Bond bag of tricks and, simultaneously, suggests the feminine identification of the father. The vial of white fluid is semen, as one would expect from the male figure of the father and, at the same time, poison, as one would expect from a dangerous CIA type. Together, of course, they represent the fearful life-threatening concept of how shattering it would be to acknowledge the buried wish for incest with the father; his semen injected into the girl would be tantamount to a death sentence.

While the injection into the arm conceals the overt sexual meaning of the act, it also represents another factor: Christine, in her anxiety to preserve her emotional distance from others, has developed a characteristic fluttering, waving-off motion of her arms. The injection into the arm could mean that she wishes for a strong man to penetrate her defenses and put a stop to this virginal flutter.

Christine, already in her thirties, divorced, a mother of children, a woman with considerable sexual experience, continues to dream of her own parents in an unmistakably sexual context. When will it stop? When will Christine start to function in her own right, totally independent of the patterns of sexual desire and guilt learned as a child and oriented toward her mother and father? Never. Nor will any of us. It appears to be the nature of the beast. We learn about sex as we learn about eating, eliminating waste, working, loving and defending ourselves from the adults who are closest to us in our childhood, and we can never completely cancel out those patterns and relationships. But when, as adults, we find ourselves behaving in a fashion that is inappropriate or destructive in sex and in personal and social relationships, we can find in our dreams the clues, the fragments from the warehouse of our mind, which tell us why we behave as we do. And, armed with the extraordinary illumination of the dark corners of our past, we can modify and moderate our present behavior and feelings.

III

SEXUAL DREAMS
and
EXISTENTIAL
ISSUES

Oedipus for the King

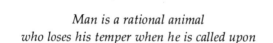

Man is a rational animal
who loses his temper when he is called upon
to act in accordance with the dictates of reason.
· OSCAR WILDE ·

Man is an intelligence in servitude to his organs.
· ALDOUS HUXLEY ·

SIMON

A Placental View

I dream that there are two unidentified people walking along as though going down a street. One of them is mocking the other. I am there, too, but in an invisible form—as a ghost. More specifically, I feel myself as a liquid presence which envelops the bodies of the two strollers. I, i.e., the liquid substance, am masturbating one of the other two people. But it is I who am enjoying the sexual sensations. It's almost as though I am having a sexual experience with a man.

Many times a millionaire, head of a financial empire known even to the casual dabbler in Wall Street, Simon is scarcely more than fifty. Attractive, athletic and in excellent health, he is happily married. He has achieved his goal of "never having to ask what anything costs," and clearly in this case, "anything" is more than a pair of shoes or the menu price of giant prawns. While we all know that "money doesn't buy happiness," most of us would be willing to give it a try. So, it is especially tempting to investigate the devils that plague the fortunate ones who do have "everything." What are their dreams? Does our successful millionaire dream happily of more success, more money, yachts, country homes, power and worldly gratifications? In fact, his dreams tend to have a troubled quality, like the dreams of most of us. Let's look at some of them.

Ghosts and Gods

This is a recurrent nightmare:

> I wake up many nights terrified by a nameless, formless presence that threatens me like a fearful spectre from a tale of Edgar Allan Poe. The apparition is vague, incorporeal, a vapor. The menace is never explicit. The shadowy horror is always around my home.

Occasionally Simon dreams of more mundane matters.

One of Our Jets Is Missing

> I am flying in a large jet. The pilot is one of the company bookkeepers. Also aboard are my partners and some other employees. The plane is flying very close to the ground and I wonder, skeptically, "When did this joker learn to fly?" Then I decide the pilot may be flying low to conserve fuel. The pilot makes a successful emergency landing on a highway right in the midst of a traffic jam. The wings and engines of the plane are at the rear and I fear they will be damaged. I warn the pilot of the danger. So the pilot

agrees to watch out but he doesn't seem very vigilant to me. When we enter a garage to ask directions, I am surprised that a couple of mechanics start to work on the plane. I hadn't supposed that anyone had had the foresight to bring mechanics along on the trip. Also, when a young woman who knows one of the partners gives us directions to the hotel where we will be staying, I complain about the character of the hotel and demand to know why we are registered at such an inferior establishment.

At the time of this dream, Simon was suffering serious, potentially diasastrous financial reverses. Yet, in his waking life, he was never known to complain or express concern. In relation to family, business associates, friends and employees, he was invariably cheerful, encouraging, positive and always ready to define adversity as a minor annoyance at worst—or even as an opportunity for gain if properly understood and exploited.

This last dream reveals his true attitude beneath the cheerful facade. He feels endangered by the pilot's (bookkeeper's) incompetence and carelessness. He is surprised that anyone has had the foresight to bring mechanics along. He is ready to complain about the inferior hotel where they must stay. To some extent then, Simon, like most dreamers, is able to use his dreams as a safety valve. If frustration is never expressed, it piles up and leads to anxiety, depression and other symptoms. The discharge function of dreams, while valuable, is not enough. That is, while dreams may help to express and relieve a dreamer's frustrations and complaints, they cannot go so far as to solve the emotional problems. To use the dream for more than the safety valve effect, the dreamer must recall the dream, understand it and put his new insight to work in his daily life. If Simon could acknowledge that it is permissible to express his discontent, dissatisfaction, criticism in his business and personal life, he would move far toward solving the problems expressed in the airplane dream. But there is surely a reason why he cannot normally voice reasonable complaints, why he must reserve them for dreams and why he is troubled by nightmares and curious, involved and sexually tangled dreams.

Simon grew up in a large northeastern city during the Great Depression. Coping with money problems was the name of the game. Both his father and mother were good at it but the father was more easygoing and even enjoyed taking time off on occasion to go to the ball park. The mother was relentlessly driving and had contempt for the father who did not quite share her single-minded devotion to the buck. But it was the son, Simon, who suffered most. He can still recall wishing at a tender age that he could come home from school to a lunch—any kind of lunch—prepared by his mother—like the other kids. Even a bologna sandwich would have been super. But mother was always too busy to provide such perquisites. Instead of the lunch (and attention) he craved, his mother would give him money to buy whatever he liked at the local café. What he recalls most clearly of long stretches of childhood was momma bitching about poppa, denigrating him as a business failure.

So eager was Simon for parental attention that he even joined the tough gang at school and was well on his way to becoming a juvenile delinquent. But that threat apparently cut no ice with momma so the boy switched and tried the opposite tack. He became a good student and graduated from high school with excellent grades. His mother wasn't impressed with that either. When Simon, on the basis of his academic achievement, decided to go to college, his mother couldn't see the point. You can't make money in school. Nor do you need a higher education to be successful. So, after only a few months, the boy cut short his college career and headed straight for Wall Street where all the money was.

During his early youth, Simon's pattern with girls was to choose a desirable one, woo her ardently until he had won her favor; then, once she was his, he lost interest in her. After driving her away with his indifference, he would again find her desirable and resume wooing her. It was only the conquest that interested him. This pattern was repeated a number of times with different women.

Flayed on a Hot Tin Hood

Now, as an adult, Simon has another frightening dream:

> A helpless animal, like a rabbit, has been skinned alive and is being eaten by a large catlike creature which stands on the hood of a car. The worst part of the dream is that the cat has absolutely no sense of the misery, pain and terror she is witlessly inflicting on her victim.

Given the many clues we already have, it seems likely that the skinned and agonized bunny is Simon preserving a child image of himself in relation to his powerful, unfeeling feline mother, who is totally unresponsive to his childish horror, pain, needs. It also seems probable that the vague miasmic nightmare that afflicts Simon is a replay of his childhood feelings of terror aroused by a rejecting mother and an inadequate father. After all, what is the nature of a child's terror in the face of parental neglect? What, concretely, does he fear? It is not so much a specific fear as a general sense of inadequacy to cope, alone, with the myriad problems that beset all of us every day, especially when we are children. When a child cannot depend on a mother to help solve his problems, it is indeed a nightmare.

This rich, powerful dreamer, this "gunslinger" whom many thousands trust with their money in the financial jungle, still lives with the child inside him, the child who is afraid to be left alone at night with the lights off. And he dares not complain in the face of the problems and adversity because this would put him in a class with his weakling father and earn the contempt of his mother.

His life is still largely devoted to trying to win the attention and affection of his mother. This is, of course, a bootless ambition. If he were as rich as Howard Hughes,

Mother would find a J. Paul Getty or an Arab oil sheik with whom to reproach him. Simon's neurotic drive will never satisfy his mother's neurotic need. Surely, it would be better for him to study his dreams, understand himself better and settle for his attractive wife, his fine children and whatever goodies a few million dollars will buy.

If there is any doubt about where momma fits into the adult Simon's feelings, let's go back to the first dream where he feels himself a liquid presence, walking down the street with two other people, one of whom is mocking the other. Simon, the liquid substance, is masturbating one of the people and getting the sexual kicks himself. Is it a homosexual dream or a dream of masturbation?

At first glance, this appears to be a homosexual dream. Simon can recall having had other homosexual dreams. But they did not disturb him because he felt no waking inclination in that direction. His *feeling* about the dream is that it is not homosexual but rather that it is a masturbation dream parading as homosexual. But why would anyone pretend to himself to have a homosexual experience, even in a dream? To cover up something even more forbidden.

While most men would probably choose to be caught masturbating rather than in *flagrante delicto* with another man, Simon is exceptionally independent and proud. He believes he would choose the homosexual act in preference to the completely autoerotic.

But something rings wrong with that kind of explanation. Perhaps we can discover better answers. After all, we're looking for something really taboo to explain the homosexual cover-up. What other clues are there? There is the other person walking along in the dream—ridiculing his/her companion. Does this fit the description of anyone in his life? Dear old mom is back in the picture throwing stones as sonny tries to have some kind, any kind, of sexual experience. Then, there is the fluid condition or cloak that makes him invisible. The last time he was invisible and walking down the street with mom, he was certainly cloaked with fluid, the fluid inside his mother's womb. The people in the dream are his mother and himself. He is having a sexual experience inside the fluid, i.e., inside his mother's womb. And that certainly seems to get to the heart of the matter.

If what Simon has in mind is a sexual go at his mother, then that certainly is taboo and had better be covered up with *anything*. The homosexual implications where he fools around with another man and has the sexual gratification himself in the dream is easier for him to accept than the notion of incest with his mother, hence the form the dream takes, the homosexual cover-up.

But Simon is not only seeking sexual contact with his mother; he is expressing that vain wish he has carried with him all these years to get under her hard and horny skin, to get her to accept him, to express love for him. Yet, even in his dream, his sharp and knowing mind censors the situation, warns him that she will laugh at him mercilessly if he tries any tricks like crawling back into the comforting amniotic fluid.

She dropped Simon into the world and told him that it's cold and harsh out here. She hasn't changed her opinion. Unfortunately, the dream is telling him the truth about her. It is also telling him the truth about himself.

And, hence, another layer of truth is disclosed by the dream: this truth is that inside Simon's own tough, capable and independent hide, the infant he once was continues to live. Simon is still part child and the realization of this offends his pride. This is another reason why he chooses to camouflage his continued sexual feelings for his mother and his dependency on her. For him, even the spectre of homosexuality is preferable to the acceptance of a degree of helplessness and infantile dependency.

Now, having wrapped these dreams into a tidy (and, we believe, accurate) package, it is time to go further. Freud demonstrated that there are endless layers of meaning in any given dream. Months on the analyst's couch can be spent associating to· any dream . . . opening doors that open onto corridors that lead ever farther back into the developmental history of the individual.

When and where is character formed? Is it at the time of the "birth shock" as some theorize? Is it at the mother's breast (or denial of it)? Is it further back in "racial memory?" Some of these hypotheses strike us as patently absurd because they ignore the obvious dynamics of life. An individual is not formed at a given moment (which is not to deny that birth shock may have an effect); nor is he formed by any single set of relationships, though some, as with the mother and father in our nuclear family, can have profound and decisive influence. An individual is continuously formed by the multiplicity of influences brought to bear during growth and development which never stop. Clearly there are influences at work at the time of birth and before that in the amniotic fluid of the womb and even before that in the genetic combinations. For if a man, through accident of his genes, inherits a dark-colored skin in a white-dominated society, no one can deny that the inherited fact of color will affect his character, point of view, emotions and inner life, as well as the objective circumstances of his life.

After birth, other genetic "accidents" will have continuing effect. Is it a boy or a girl? How do the parents feel about the child's sex, eye color, hair? Some like it curly; some like it straight. Beyond that, the child will be influenced by uncountable factors in the home. Are the parents happy together? Rich or poor? Struggling or content? Fiercely competitive, frustrated, displacing ambition unfairly on a child, wanting him to be an intellectual, a doctor, a baseball pitcher—which poppa never got a chance to be? Is the child growing up in a society that dignifies labor or guilt-edged securities? Is it a society that glorifies war, prescribes religion, threatens hell and damnation, proscribes sexuality? Are there brothers and sisters? Is death witnessed routinely or hidden away with fear and shame? Do the opinion-makers believe that all problems of mankind can be solved by the application of human intelligence and diligence? Do they take their small sons, as Lincoln Steffens did, show him a leaking faucet and point out that it is a true and good destiny for man to go forward to fix not only the plumbing but the health, welfare and faulty social contracts of civilization?

Or is the world ruled by shamen who teach that the earth and the heavens were created in final form aeons ago and the puny efforts of man are ever doomed to futility? All these attitudes and influences act upon the developing individual like a bombardment of cosmic rays that penetrate the atmosphere and the skin and skull which sheathe the brain. All these influences leave an indelible imprint on the mind, which is not only the brain but the entire nervous system interacting with the skin and bones and feet and colon and reproductive system, with the liver and the ductless glands and with the literally billions of cells of which we are built. All these things are at work in the unique mind of the unique individual which each of us is.

What has all this to do with dreams? The dream is a one-man show, an exclusively personal production like none other in human experience. The dreamer is the author, actor, director, producer. He is in charge of the wardrobe, special effects and makeup. He creates faces to cover up faces if it suits his purpose. He can arrange for the same actor (frequently himself) to play more than one role. He is the imaginative film editor leaping improbably from sequence to sequence. He is the entrepreneur, the theatre owner, the one who provides the film, the projectionist and, finally, the audience. No Fellini, no Ingmar Bergman, no David Lean can approach the dreamer's resources and absolute control of the medium. And into this fantastic production with unlimited budget, into this dream, he brings everything he is, everything that has happened to him, that he fears and wishes.

Simon felt, justly, that his mother had neglected him as a child. He was hostile to her and insecure because of her; but he continued to need her approval. These are seemingly contradictory attitudes. Yet, they can be encompassed, and usually are, within the single complex fabric of the unconscious. There is still another and more forceful contradiction revealed in the dreams. If we look closely, we will find that the son also *became* the mother. He emulated her to win her approval. He emulated her because he grew up in a world which glorified her values. But he didn't become exactly like her because the bombardment of influences that penetrated his skin and skull for more than forty years were not identically the same as those to which she had been exposed. In fact, he became much more successful than she. But his dreams reveal that he also developed misgivings about his social role. He feels guilty about his hunger for wealth and power. The great devouring feline beast munching on the flayed rabbit is not only Simon's mother; it is also Simon himself. Walk through another looking glass and study the picture from another angle. The suffering bunny is, indeed, Simon, but it is also Simon's real life victims. This gunslinger has a very active conscience. He works seriously to do good deeds, cultural and social, with his wealth. He grew up, remember, in an economic depression when ideas of social justice were abroad and he lived through the "war to end wars."

His recurrent vague nightmare was, we said, a reflection of childhood anxiety when he felt he had no mother to protect him. But this dream also reflects his fear of punishment for the role he plays in society. In part, he sees himself as an accumulator of wealth (at whose expense?) and suffers a vague but persistent conviction that some awful retribution will be visited upon him.

There is no rule in dreams that only a single interpretation, a single answer, is correct. There is no true or false test. It is a multiple-answer test where all the choices may be correct. Examine the dream as you would a drop of good milk. We say the milk is pure and healthful. That is true. But though it is fresh and pasteurized, examination under the microscope reveals multitudes of bacteria which have not been destroyed. That is also true and not necessarily contradictory. Continue to magnify with an electron microscope and we begin to see how much more complex the simple drop of milk becomes, reflecting in its organic chemistry the problems basic to life. These things are true, too. Going still further, into its molecules, the milk reflects the matter and energy equations of the universe. This represents another level of "truth." Just as a drop of milk or water may be endlessly explored for meaning, so can the single dream of a man or woman be used as a key to the endless variety and richness of the individual's history.

In practice, we do not find it necessary or practical to squeeze all of the meaning out of a single dream. It is more useful to take them as they come. Meaningful patterns will invariably recur. A "lost" or forgotten dream is only shoved back into the inventory. You will find it there on the shelf when you need it again and are ready to use it.

The inherent complexity of dreams may seem daunting. But to stop trying to understand dreams because of their richness would be like refusing to drink milk because of its infinite content. A glass of milk, to paraphrase Freud, is also a glass of milk. A dream, even if not fully explored, is also a lovely revelation of the inner self.

The
Masochistic Woman

Backward, turn backward, O Time, in thy flight;
Make me a child again, just for tonight.
· ELIZABETH AKERS ALLEN ·

ELLA

Svidrigailov's Dream

I am with my attorney in a cavernous apartment like a
Chelsea studio; but it is the lawyer's office and it is a catastrophic mess. My attorney and I appear to be in the midst
of a legal conference, but we are laughing and having fun
like buddies. A little girl is there, pathetic, thin, raggedy. I
make love to the little girl but I cannot recall any details of
this. When it is over, I put my arm around the child and
ask, "Was that good for you?" The little girl replies, "No, I
can't come with all the people and interruptions." I then
tell the child that I, too, was unable to come.

On waking, Ella was initially horrified that she had been homosexual and, particularly, that she had seduced a child. She had indeed been the aggressor, the man. In puberty, Ella had a homosexual experience with an older sister who seduced her and who reached a sexual climax during the episode. The sister's orgasm seemed so wild that it frightened Ella. When another sister proposed sex, Ella flatly turned her down; she was going to have nothing more to do with that scary stuff. Many years after the youthful and isolated event, Ella had a love affair with a man who was primarily homosexual. After he had left her for a man, Ella was very hurt and she let an older woman make love to her.

Married now for a number of years, Ella has become emotionally detached from her husband in order, as she sees it, to protect herself from his chronic hostility. In her dependence on her attorney of whom she dreamed and to whom she turns for advice, she has become sexually attached. There is no love affair but, in the privacy of her thoughts, she wishes for one. This wish is one source of the dream. She also feels continuing guilt over the homosexual episodes in her life and she has never fully recovered from the trauma of her sexual seduction by her older sister. Both factors contribute to the homosexual part of the dream. But it is more significant to understand that the little girl in the dream is Ella herself and that she is "fucking" herself. Ella has an earthy sense of humor and a vocabulary to match, so this is exactly how she would put it. The "fucking" is not the autoerotic variety, not sexual; it is a vivid metaphor of her lifelong problem of self-depreciation. She continually puts herself down. This masochism is what appears in the dream. At one time, when she was an aspiring writer, new to the big city, she had an apartment filled with books, music and art, very romantic and like the atmosphere in the dream. The dialogue in the dream comes to mean, in paraphrase: "Is it good for me to fuck myself in life? No, it is not rewarding, not fulfilling, not good for me to be self-destructive in my life."

Ella was born into a lower middle-class family in the South. There were a number of sisters and brothers. Although the family had a conventional facade, the father was an unstable man who was often the source of embarrassment and financial difficulty. The mother, despite her strict Southern Baptist religion, had a lusty streak in her humor and language which Ella adored. Although the father depreciated Ella and her sisters, the mother respected their femininity, recognized Ella's artistic gifts and encouraged her in her writing as an escape from the destructive pressures of the family. By late adolescence, Ella was gone to the city. By twenty, she had her first disastrous love affair with a much older man. A few years later, she married. This marriage has endured but principally because of Ella's stubborn determination not to let it go down the drain.

Her dream is like a distorting mirror that underscores and emphasizes a number of the themes of Ella's life problems: it shows a healthy wish for a relaxed and enjoyable sex life with a man (the attorney); a latent homosexual wish; a wish (or need) to be "fucked over" in life; continuing guilt and trauma from childhood sexuality involving her sisters; it also shows her making love to a child who is herself and, therefore, saying: If no one else will love her, she must reluctantly provide her own love for herself.

There are some intriguing unanswered questions about the dream. Why, for example, was the attorney's office a "catastrophic mess" rather than the clean pleasant place it actually is? Does this suggest a latent fear of the man with whom, in the dream, she professes to feel so relaxed, happy and secure? And why does she have no recall of the sex with the little girl? Is that the clue that basically it did not represent sex but was a metaphor of her masochism; or was the sexual detail repressed even in the dream due to Ella's intense guilt and shame over perverse sexuality? We do not know the answers to these questions. No person seriously examining his dreams can expect a complete analysis of any one dream, however simple it may appear.

But this dream is enormously useful because it clearly highlights a number of the problems which Ella must probe, and promising because it shows she is facing up to some of the painful areas of feeling that she has long repressed.

As further dreams will demonstrate, Ella is not merely a woman with problems, she is a gifted and dynamic person who can recount a variety of interesting dreams on a variety of subjects. Certainly, she knows pain (isn't that the human condition?), but she also has the wit and humor that set humans apart from rocks and spinach and mosquitoes and baboons.

Doctor Sexinger

I am in a large house with my sister, Georgia. I am in bed with Henry Kissinger and, as I inspect and fondle him, I realize that he has breasts like a cow's teats or human baby penises. But that all seems perfectly natural. We fool around for a while but we never really get going sexually. It's vague, but then he leaves, irritated. At first I'm puzzled but then I assume he's angry because I have a date with Richard Nixon. I am frustrated because I wanted to have sex and I tell Georgia that her hovering around the bed hadn't helped things any with Henry. Now my mother is with me; she sort of pushes me into a dance, and it quickly becomes a sexual embrace. As we dance, mother is in the position of the male dancer and moving her body against mine very provocatively. Then she seems to be urging me to ingratiate myself with Nixon. But I don't want to; still, I feel I can't oppose her wishes directly, so I try to divert mother's interest by discussing the decor of the house. I awaken.

Ella is quite a big girl now. At forty, she works as a magazine editor and competes successfully in the tough arena of journalism. She feels that if she were not handicapped by being a woman, she would achieve much more. She and her husband have a large circle of friends, including many at the top of the social ladder. Ella is surprised and amused that despite her regular association with the great and glamorous, she still dreams of being in their intimate company like an adolescent star-struck girl. Actually, she dislikes Henry Kissinger, thinks he's power mad, so why the wish to screw him? To be sure, her sexual desire for him in the dream is not undiluted; she simultaneously mocks him by picturing him as a freakish hermaphrodite, by indicating that she has a more important rendezvous with Richard Nixon and by leaving him sexually unsatisfied and irritated. She also seems to be casting more doubt on his male identity by giving him breasts like baby-sized penises which may open to question his vaunted ladies' man image. Dr. Kissinger is getting quite a working over but it's probably nothing personal. Ella is working out deeper problems which appear when her mother replaces Kissinger in the dream as the object of Ella's sexual interest.

Ella's mother was the stable, dependable parent, and Ella loved her deeply. This dependent, trusting love became sexualized—as do all human relationships; thus, her mother becomes her lover in the dream. But, though Ella undeniably and evidently loved her mother, this love was not unalloyed. It was complicated by other factors; the mother made onerous demands on Ella. She required the girl, at too early an age, to assume many burdensome responsibilities. For this, Ella has always harbored feelings of bitterness that go back to her most youthful years. And, to this day, she pictures her mother coercing her into a role (courting Richard Nixon) which runs counter to her wishes. Ella's sister is there, too, interfering with Ella's love life—as she undoubtedly did in childhood when she competed with Ella for mother's attention (as well as involving her in a homosexual episode).

The picture we get of Ella from this dream is that unconsciously (1) she does wish to court and seduce powerful male figures like Henry Kissinger but (2) she simultaneously needs to mock them, reduce them down in size, that (3) she has a powerful sexual feeling for her mother, but

(4) she resents her mother and (5) she has not quite forgiven her sister for coming between her and her mother. All of this adds up, among other things, to a confusion of sexual identity. Does Ella really want to play the game as a woman or as a man? All this is consistent with the texture of her first dream about the homosexual encounter with the little ragamuffin girl.

Ella continues to dream:

A Surgical Cure

> I am in love with a man; we make marvelous love. Then, I realize there is something monstrously wrong with his cock. He must have surgery because of this abnormality. He is in a place like a big antique store where I can see him but I can't reach him. An older woman is there; she seems to be in charge and she treats me as though I were naughty to make love to the man.

Again, she enjoys sex with a man but, again, there is something wrong about him sexually and physically. Again, too, a mother figure appears and takes over. Ella dreams some more:

Hermes or Aphrodite

> A man is standing, completely naked. He doesn't notice me at all. He has a large penis, but just below the penis is an umbrella sticking out of his body. It is closed but it is like a female opening. The man seems proud.

The hermaphrodite appears again. The man has a large penis and another odd appendage that's like a "female opening." All of these dreams express Ella's protest at the dominance of men. She deforms the men in her dreams, particularly caricaturing their sexuality in order to equalize the situation. She perceives the world as a place where men have unfair advantages over women, and she's out to redress the balance.

Is it true what they say about penis envy? Yes, but the concept has been so vulgarized as to border on the ridiculous. We know that women envy men in our world; and we know that men have many important advantages handed to them automatically—simply because they are men. It's men who are the priests in most of our religions; men who are the generals; men who wield the essential economic and political power; men who get the gravy in the arts, sciences and professions; men who go first to the moon. We know that when women are still little girls, they are alert to which sex is the boss in the home—and outside. Since, for all the world, it appears that the most significant difference between the sexes is the appendage which the man has between his legs, it's reasonable for women to attach their envy of men's social advantages to the penis. Does it go deeper than this? Perhaps. We really don't know. We do know that there are male-female differences in the animal and insect world where social causation does not operate in the same way. We don't know how lady lions (who do the hunting) feel about the penises of male lions, who do the best eating (and, on rare occasion, the fighting). We don't know how the male mantis feels about the female mantis as she munches off his head even while he is completing the act of copulation with her. Certainly, we don't know how women would feel about the penis in a society where there was no social discrimination against women. But, in our society, there is penis envy, and Ella has her share of it.

If Ella shows her sexual identity conflict more than most, it's because she has an exceptionally keen and searching mind which is prepared, even in her dreams, to tackle painful truths. Ella has begun to understand the particular influences that affected her while she was growing up. Her mother was strong, and she identified with her; her father was weak (so where did he come off to flaunt his pendulous prerogatives?). There is one fragment that comes back from the "forgotten" past as Ella thinks about the penis-umbrella dream; she recalls that when she was four or five, her father threatened to cut off her ear if she continued to ignore her mother's calls for her to come in from play. If daddy could cut off her ear so easily, perhaps somewhere in the past someone cut off a penis she was born with. Women frequently have this fantasy.

Nor should we forget that Ella is in a profession where men make most of the rules, decisions and money. She's tired of the unfairness. So, in her dreams, Ella has declared war on female segregation. She's demanding busing, an end to the poll tax, slum clearance—the whole bit (but for women). It looks as though, in life, she's going to get at least some of what she wants (so, *caveat* Henry Kissinger).

As if she didn't already have enough problems, it must also be noted that Ella is exceptionally attractive and voluptuous and she feels this has helped her to climb over the usual obstacles strewn in the path of a career woman. But, if she has used the accident of her comeliness to make points in love and work, this same factor becomes a source of anxiety when at the age of forty she begins to think of losing her beauty. So, Ella dreams:

The Seat of Her Trouble

> I am at my dresser searching for a pair of my satin panties and can't find them. I'm sure my daughter has taken them and this angers me. I wonder why she can't be satisfied with her cotton panties since she is only an adolescent. The scene changes. I am now in my gynecologist's waiting room which is large and crowded. I have an appointment to see him. A girl in her teens is in the seat which is the appropriate one for me. I brusquely insist that the girl relinquish the seat and she does obey me.

Now that she is entering her fifth decade, Ella experiences the commonly felt dread of women in our culture. Is she still sexually desirable? How long will it last? The legitimate personal aspirations and complaints are distorted by the endless male-female warfare which engulfs her and the rest of us.

Cannibalism
and Black Sex

Those that want friends to open themselves unto
are cannibals of their own hearts.
· FRANCIS BACON ·

GREG

Cannibalism

> Two beautifully formed children who remind me of my
> own fair-skinned daughters have died. There is a group of
> adults nearby who are very hungry and they are preparing
> to bake the children in an oven with the intention of eating
> them. I am attempting to protect my wife from knowledge
> of all this.

Greg is a married man in his middle thirties. The dream
occurred immediately after Greg and his wife had spent a

weekend with several other couples whom he regards as disturbed. They are sexually promiscuous, use large amounts of marijuana (and possibly other drugs) and are constantly in search of kicks. Greg believes the dream in some way reflects his own weakness, his willingness to go along under social pressure with activities alien to his own standards. On this weekend, contrary to his real inclinations, he almost became sexually involved with one of the aggressive women. He felt resentfully that his wife colluded with the others to promote the almost successful seduction.

As Greg thought about the dream of eating the children, he felt frightened. All his life he has felt guilt, even about having been born. His maternal grandmother, who reared him from the ages of one to five, told him how he was conceived out of wedlock, how the pregnancy forced marriage on the poor, young and emotionally immature mother and father. She filled his ears with horror stories: there was never any food for him to eat except some cereal; he became asthmatic by the age of six months, had mastoiditis and a mastoidectomy; by the time he was a year old, he was suffering from severe pneumonia. The grandmother told him his parents fought incessantly, neglected his diet, health and emotional needs to such a point that when she and his grandfather rescued him at the age of one, he was malnourished and sickly and in danger of dying. Greg is still horrified when he considers the slim thread of luck by which he hung onto life. He could have been scraped out of his mother's womb through an illegal abortion and flushed down the toilet; his mother, illegitimately pregnant, could have suicided; or he could have died from illness, malnutrition or neglect in infancy.

After he was five or six, his mother reclaimed him. She was a very pretty, intelligent and seductive woman who had passed through a series of husbands and lovers. Greg, early on, learned to fend for himself. He became an outstanding student and quite "independent." Perforce, he accepted the arrival of some new half-brothers. Between men, his mother would move closer to Greg, her firstborn, but when she found a new love, he would again experience a profound sense of loss and anxiety. Since he had had almost no contact with his father from the age of one, there was also a hope that he would find another father with each new man who came into the house. But these hopes were invariably dashed by the succession of self-preoccupied men who paraded through his mother's life.

When he was in his late adolescence, Greg's hopes for reunion with his natural father were destroyed by a letter from relatives telling him that his father had recently died of acute cancer. This terrible event plunged Greg into a depression from which he has never fully recovered.

Why, now, does he dream of cannibalism; why, particularly, does he dream of his own well-loved children subjected to this horror? There is, for starters, a remarkably consistent tendency for parents to identify narcissistically with their young children, i.e., they love the children as they love themselves, as they wish they had been loved when they were young. When you encounter your own or any young children in a dream, you are likely to discover that it is a phase of yourself you are portraying. Greg, who suffered so painfully and so long during his childhood, has good reason to hate the memories of pain and misery. Unfortunately, this hate becomes directed against himself as though the miserable little boy back there had been responsible for the suffering. Children who are damaged so painfully take upon themselves the guilt for their own misery. They don't know who else to blame. They don't learn to love themselves in a normal healthy way but come to hate themselves, instead. In dreaming of the children, dead and cannibalized, his own children, himself, Greg is struggling to cast out the devils of his own childhood which continue to plague him. Cannibalism reflects self-hate at its rawest.

The dream of cannibalism was a watershed dream; it marked Greg's change of attitude toward himself. He had never before dreamed of his wife. Apparently, he was now

becoming ready to look realistically for the first time at his wife, his marriage, his family life and himself. So, approximately two weeks later he dreamed the following:
ing:

Black Sex

> I am driving my convertible along the ocean road, planning to visit friends, feeling carefree. Then, I am in the parking lot of an office building where I work. I leave the car and, as I pass through a corridor, I notice a room which is like a barroom. There are many blacks, men and women, all dancing in a very sexual way. One woman is bare-breasted, undulating provocatively. She thrusts her great breasts toward me; I start to taste them, to suck. I feel very sexual. Then, the dance is over and I feel pleasantly excited. A man and woman are dancing nude, touching each other's bodies. The man has a very long tongue with which he licks his thighs, pelvis and lower abdomen in order to lubricate his body where it makes contact with the woman's. She is also well greased. While they continue their fascinating insectlike dance, I leave the room. Then I am in my car again talking with an accountant who is older and who is one of my bosses. This other accountant tells me that his daughter was the woman whose breast I was sucking. It turns out to be a most pleasant and genial conversation.

Is there any connection between the cannibalism dream and the dream of black sex? One may, of course, recall that the association of the average person to cannibalism is the cartoon image of a group of black Africans surrounding an enormous simmering stewpot in which a couple of white captives are making bad jokes. But the second dream is very different in feeling from the first. The cannibalism dream was extremely disturbing; the dream of black sex was pleasant and wishful. In this second dream, there is great emphasis on the exaggerated sexuality of the blacks, a common white stereotype. The woman does not just have breasts, but "great breasts"; she is "provocative, undulating"; they are all dancing in a very "sexual way"; the black man has an extraordinary tongue, so long that he can touch his own thighs, pelvis, abdomen with it while dancing. The tongue is certainly a substitute for the enormous penis with which most whites endow most blacks. In his unconscious, at least, Greg is a victim of the same clichés that whites associate with black sex. Black sex is supersex. If you want to dream of wild, free, sexy sex, you can dream of black sex for the same price. So, in the second dream, Greg is trying out a freer lubricious sex. He is trying to free himself of the limitations, inhibitions, taboos, uptightness with which he habitually approaches sex. He even invents for himself an improbable situation where the black dancer, whose splendid breast he sucks, turns out to be the daughter of the senior partner in his firm who, a white, genially informs Greg that the black girl with whom he has been indulging himself is actually his daughter. It is all very pleasant, friendly, relaxed. Evidently, Greg is telling himself wishfully that it is all right to indulge in sex more freely. Even the authority figures will approve.

The dreams seem to be connected in the following sense: Greg is saying, "If I tackle my self-hate and my image of myself as a bad child who deserves to be destroyed and devoured by unfeeling adults, then I will rid myself of the guilt and self-punishment that prevent me from enjoying life more and, specifically, from enjoying a more liberated and entertaining sex life."

Alienation:
Sexual and Social

---◦⦿◦---

*Oh God! I could be bounded in a nutshell
and count myself a king of infinite space,
were it not that I have bad dreams.*

· HAMLET ·

STAN

Trouble with Naked Girls

I dream that there are two naked girls. One seems as
though she must be a girl I have loved or wanted to love or
may still love though I can give her no name. The other is
an even younger girl I have just met. They both seem willing to have sexual relations with me and there is a hint of
pleasure on my part that they may even be jealous of each
other over me. I am aware of my age in the dream, that I
am a man in his fifties and that both of these girls are
young and desirable.

I decide that I will skip the games with the younger girl
and make a rendezvous with the other one, the one I am in

love with. As we leave the room where we have been and start through what appears to be a courtyard, the younger girl provocatively stops short in front of me so that I bump squarely into her attractive bare buttocks. There is a pleasurable sensation as my genitals come into contact with her naked flesh, nothing very exciting—just mildly pleasurable. Perhaps I am reminded of the lovely fleshly things I am giving up in rejecting this girl but my mind is on the important rendezvous with the other girl who is much more important to me.

Now the younger girl disappears from the dream and I follow a few lengths behind the other girl who is heading toward my room and the rendezvous. I notice that there are a number of young men, about twenty years of age, sitting around on the pavement of the courtyard, a sunny place, playing some kind of game. I think of a game like "marbles" that kids would play on the ground but these young men are too mature for that. Perhaps they are shooting craps, though in the dream it is not specific nor does it appear to be anything as tough and adult as craps. My girl now approaches the outside wall of my apartment; for a reason never explained, she cannot get in through the door [no door? no key?] but must climb up into my room through the window that faces the courtyard. I notice briefly when she bends as though to look for a step or a purchase to get up and through the window, that her breasts are larger than I expected and flaccid. But it is only a fleeting observation.

The girl will clearly have difficulty getting up and through the window which opens high above where she can reach. One of the young men (they have paid no particular attention to us) politely offers to help her so she can get through the window. I notice that he has a fine shock of dark hair; his offer of help is friendly, not competitive, not leering. But my reaction is that I cannot let someone else, certainly not such a strong young man, interpose himself here and help the girl to *my* rendezvous. I am now keenly aware of my age. To rely on the young man's help would be to confess my infirmity. It would be demeaning.

So I wave him away, lace my fingers together and hold my hands as a stirrup for the girl to step on. She obliges. I try. I find her surprisingly heavy and have the greatest difficulty boosting all of her weight. It is a severe struggle and I am afraid I will drop her altogether, fail to get her high enough to get into my room. I will be humiliated if this happens. I strain mightily, raising my hands and the girl higher until her foot is at a level with my chest. But this still is not enough and the whole situation threatens to collapse farcically. I make a final mighty effort and virtually fling her up and through the window. This works so well that she plunges through the window, falls on her head inside and is knocked out. For my part, the exertion has taxed my last resources and I fall into a dead faint outside at the foot of the wall. So much for my rendezvous.

Stan is a man in his fifties with thinning hair and the usual sexual anxieties of his age. When he wakes up from this dream, he is amused by the silly figure he has cut and by the obviousness of the content. He knows about his age, about his anxieties and he knows there are no attractive naked young women vying for his favors. He knows all of this perfectly well in his waking life and doesn't need a dream to tell it to him and poke fun at him. He is puzzled about why his unconscious has bothered to present this situation in such rich detail just to remind him of what he already knows. Perhaps it is simply a safety valve for his fears and inner conflicts in the area of sex.

But Stan feels that there may be more to the dream than he comprehends. He does find the dream amusing and doesn't hesitate to tell it to his wife and to others. He doesn't feel especially defensive about his sexual performance. But only after Stan remembers that when he was a young man of about twenty he had a thick shock of dark hair does he recognize that the helpful young fellow in the dream was himself. So, the dream takes on another dimension. He is not merely facing his declining sexuality, he is saying to himself that he is, in fact, no longer the young buck with lots of dark hair and the muscles he once had and that he should stop making a silly ass of himself, hoping for love affairs with young girls who can certainly get a bigger boost out of young men (of the type he once was).

Stan is evidently going through an emotional menopause, unwilling to accept the fact of his aging, still with
an inner image of himself as a physically desirable male
—until the dream holds up an ironic mirror in which he
can not only see himself more clearly but see himself in
contrast to what he once was. But the dream offers the
man a consolation prize; it says that it is true that you are
not the man, sexually, you once were, but don't make
such a tragedy of it; after all, you did have your day.

Will this dream help Stan accept the painful "facts of
life?" Probably no single dream or insight or encounter or
experience is enough to achieve acceptance and adjustment to sometimes painful reality. But the dream adds its
soupçon of truth, its sharp and wry focus on the situation
and, when studied and understood, can help toward a
kind of adjustment. Certainly, the fact that he can see himself in his dream as a comic figure bodes well. It should
help him to diminish the earnestness with which he tends,
in waking, to view the unpalatable truth.

In discussing analytic therapy, Freud acknowledged
that treatment cannot always help a person to attain his
wishes. There are obvious limits since many of us wish to
be young when we're old; tall when we're short; men
when we're women (and vice versa); some of us, no
doubt, even want to pass through the needle's eye when
we're big as camels. There are limits to what treatment—
or dream interpretation—can accomplish. But, happily,
one can learn to renounce unattainable desires with good
grace—and good humor.

Underlying the problem of aging, though, there exists
the more basic question of sexual potency. There is no reason why a man in his fifties can't "get it up" as seems to be
the situation in Stan's dream. Stan does, in fact, intermittently experience problems of impotence, premature ejaculation, flat orgasm—the works. The reasons for this will
be examined; but the connection we find most meaningful
in Stan's case is to his career, work, life-style. Stan is an
example of the middle-class middle intellectual with every
outward sign of success. Yet he is most dissatisfied and his

problems of sexual inadequacy are mirrored in every aspect of his work and career. Not because he is typical but because he does represent and sum up a very familiar set of emotional problems that will find an uneasy echo in many others, we think it worthwhile to explore more of his dreams and probe their meaning. In this instance, the direct sexual dream about the two naked girls is only a prelude to a series of other dreams which extend the area in which we may explore not only Stan's sexual problems but the closely related personal problems and his perception of the world which is the same world that presses in on all of us.

At this point in his career, Stan is an executive in one of the rattiest of the rat races, television. He started as a radio and television writer, was good enough to work on some of the more important shows and moved up to production. For years he has been attached as an assistant and associate to a freewheeling high-level operator, a real promoter who puts shows and packages together. We'll call this second man "B" for barracuda. Stan dreams:

The White Mouse Connection

I am involved in some activity with B and learn to my surprise that B is in the midst of a major Broadway theatrical venture. My feelings about this are a mixture of anger that B has proceeded so far into the production without having let me know about it and admiration that, despite all the other projects and the difficulties with which we are presently beset, B has been so enterprising as to put together a Broadway production. Now, B requires me to do a strange chore. The location is the interior of my car but it is an unusual car with no seats or interior fittings; it is like a small empty room. Inside this car are a couple of white mice. I am told to hook these mice to a set of low-voltage electrical wires that will activate their muscles in a certain fashion and make it appear that they are running in a normal manner. With the first pair of mice, it seems that I am instructed and guided by B so that the hookup does work satisfactorily. Even so, I am queasy about it; I don't know whether this process may be painful for the mice, and there is something objectionable about forcing these poor little helpless creatures to perform without their free will like puppets in response to the electricity.

But it gets still worse because then I must hook up another pair of white mice by myself. B is impatient; he must get going (back to the theatrical production?); and I have to hurry in order to go along with him. Yet, I must complete this second hookup all by myself as though the first pair have only been for demonstration purposes. I can't seem to get the wiring right. The poor mice never fight back; they permit me to connect the wires uncomplainingly, then lie there quivering erratically. B doesn't give a damn about how the mice feel; he just wants to get going but I keep hanging back, wanting to straighten out the wires because I am afraid the mice may be suffering.

Stan, like most people in our world, feels a profound and continuing resentment toward his work. Both the psychologists and sociologists label this feeling "alienation." Whether he works in a mine, a factory, a supermarket, a medical clinic or for a television network, a man (or woman) feels that the best part of his life, most of every working day, is taken from him and simply appropriated for someone else's gain (the employer, the company, etc.). It is not basically that the worker feels inadequately paid, not that he feels his work is dull and meaningless, but that he objects to the power of others (whether personal or impersonal) to force him to work and live for someone else's existential benefit. So pervasive is this sense of alienation that it appears to affect equally the highly paid television writer functioning under the profit system and the farmer in the Soviet Union who dogs it during his assigned workday on the collective farm only to pitch in with enthusiasm when he is raising cucumbers for private sale on his own garden plot.

Like many others who work without personal satisfaction in the intellectual and cultural slums, Stan suffers a triple hex: first, there is the familiar alienation because his work is for the benefit of others; second, he feels that whatever talent he may have is corrupted by the commercial demands of the mass media and, third, he knows that he is participating in a gigantic system of bread and circuses, lulling the public into a torpid acceptance of the status quo, keeping them glued to the tube for most of their free hours while beady-eyed hustlers of every description (manufacturers, merchants, service organizations, politicians, lawyers, doctors) rob them blind. Wars are organized, inflation is rigged and depression is tolerated while Stan's audience stares hypnotized at the images Stan creates of good cops trapping bad crooks in an endless series of happy endings.

So, Stan dreams. The helpless white mice with whom he identifies so touchingly can readily be seen to represent Stan himself (micelf). He sees himself as a helpless and unprotesting puppet in B's power and he is so trapped by the system that he cooperates even to the extent of connecting the tormenting wires himself! The mice also represent all the victims of B's machinations, including the television audience which is corrupted by his electronic productions, while Stan, however reluctant, goes along doing B's bidding, tormenting and damaging the victims because he cannot resist B's authority and promises of rewards (the Broadway production). The parable of Stan's real life situation was not less pointed because it took place inside his automobile, a classic Bentley, of which he is reluctantly proud.

Even in his dream it appears that Stan cannot quite unload all the blame for what is happening on B. In addition to being present as the victim (the mice), Stan is also there in person, playing an important role; he is the one who is performing a hands-on job of tormenting the mice with the electric (electronic? television?) wires. The dream seems to be saying: "Come out from behind that self-pitying camouflage and recognize your own responsibility for what you do. You tell yourself that B is the villain and that you are merely an unwilling tool; that all guilt should be laid at the feet of the conniving promoter who generates all the schemes; that you, Stan, reserve for yourself a feeling of moral superiority because you go along under protest and you understand the moral equation, because you are more sensitive and refuse to deny that wrong is being done. This is how you escape a full sense of culpability." The dream rubs Stan's nose into the situation, portraying clearly that he is a full partner in B's antimouse operations. If he examines the implications of his own dream honestly, Stan will not be able to hide behind the rationalizations which have given him some comfort (and a great deal of inner conflict).

We have chosen, in order to illustrate the problems of alienation at work, to emphasize the social extension of this dream. Does this mean that there is no latent sexual content? Clearly, there is. Stan's passive-aggressive feelings for his powerful associate reveal an unease about sexual identity for Stan. He plays a distinctly feminine role in relation to B and he resists this bitterly. This colors his reaction to work and authority and compounds the alienation syndrome. We have seen, earlier, that he suffers intermittently from sexual impotence; now we perceive other forms of impotence relating to his work, to his career associations and to his view of what he may not be doing about the problems he sees in the world around him.

Alienation is perceived by the sociologist, who focuses on the nature of the work relationship in a given society, and also by the psychologist, who is more concerned with the complex interrelation of social and personal factors which give rise to alienation. But whatever the discipline of the observer, it is broadly agreed that alienation exists as a pervasive emotional malaise, and it is worth examining apart from its sexual implications. In our culture, whether a person is a baker, a boxer, a secretary or a mother and housewife, alienation is certain to show up in life and in dreams.

The same night, after the mouse dream, Stan returned to sleep and had another dream:

The Adding Machine Murder

Someone has been murdered. I am charged with investigating the murder. Some clever soul has determined that the essential clue resides in an adding machine tape. I must go around to a great number of business offices to check adding machine tapes to see if any of them will yield a clue to the murderer's identity. I go from office to office and am met apprehensively. I explain that I do not expect to find any suspects among the people in these offices; I am only looking for adding machines. I manage to collect a number of tapes and examine them for the obscure clue which I seem to recall looks like a shorthand character.

Regarding the manifest content of the dream, all the busyness with offices, adding machines, tapes, numbers and shorthand characters appear to be the "day residue" of the commercial activities in which Stan and B were involved. But what about the murder? Who killed Cock Robin? And who *is* Cock Robin? The dead person has no identity. No one, including the dreamer, has any concern on that score. The very impersonality of the killing, that it occurred offscene, that there are no images to support it, suggests that we are dealing with a generality, murder in a general sense, as we speak of genocide. The fact that the essential clue must be found on an adding machine tape is interestingly specific. Add to this Stan reassuring the people in the offices that he does not expect to find the killer among them, that he is only interested in tapes— and it begins to look as though the "murder" was actually committed by an adding machine! This introduces the equation: adding machine equals murder. The adding machine is, of course, a fine symbol for all business. In business, properly conducted for profit, most human factors are eliminated; everything is reduced to numbers, percentage returns, markups, depreciation, overhead, cash flow, etc. A company's annual statement relies heavily on the services of an adding machine; it does not provide information about how many people were made happy or unhappy by the conduct of business during the course of the fiscal year.

Given Stan's bias about business, it appears that the dream is saying, "If you remain in the writing *business* with B, you will be committing murder by adding machine. Perhaps the victim of the murder will be Stan himself or his talent; perhaps, in view of his bad conscience, the murdered person may stand in a general way for all the poor victims exposed daily and nightly to his programs. In any event, it seems that Stan is telling himself that it is wrong (as murder is wrong) to continue in this commercialized form of writing. Again, we have the deep, even morbid sense of the man's alienation from his work. And, again, we could play interesting games with the latent sexual content. The adding machine tape is an unusual elongated piece of paper and might suggest a phallic shape; but, if so, it is a phallus without any rigidity. Is Stan searching for an answer to his lack of sexual firmness? Such speculations would have to be answered in relation to Stan's own associations to the dream. Here, we are intent on focusing on the social alienation which is so prevalent and destructive among us.

Stan did have an interesting association to these dreams, possibly triggered by the electrified mice of the first dream. Since childhood, Stan had had a recurrent nightmare of execution in the electric chair.

Electrocution Fits the Crime

The details did not vary significantly, always a version of being led down the "last mile" through the little door into the execution chamber. The last time the dream had occurred, Stan was an adult, only a year or two before the dreams reported above. This time:

> I am condemned again and waiting in a prison cell, chatting with a good friend and fellow writer. We both know that our execution is approaching but we continue to talk in animated fashion without being especially concerned about our approaching doom.
>
> Suddenly we are confonted by guards who hustle the two of us and two other condemned wretches out of the cell where we have been chatting so cozily despite the realization that our time is running out. Thus far, the dream has not been especially unpleasant, just that dread

and heavy sense of death waiting close by, a sense that I am familiar with from the recurrent nightmare. The four of us are now herded roughly into another cell which is clearly the antechamber of the execution room. Here, the only really nasty thing happens. As we are all shoved inside, a brutal guard who is dressed in a kind of loose oriental kimono, grabs each of us and throws us into a corner in a heap, one on top of the other. There seems to be no excuse for this brutality. The room is empty; the doors are locked. There is nothing that any of us can do to rebel, resist or escape. I merely sense in the dream that it must be official policy to intimidate us with senseless brutality just in case any of us should have a spirited notion to make trouble at the last moment. In the dream, I feel oppressed by the sense of man's limitless inhumanity. How can you bully anyone more vulnerable than a poor bastard who is about to be strapped into the electric chair? And what purpose could it serve?

In thinking about the dream, Stan was able to trace elements back to a number of circumstances in his childhood. First, there had been a great deal of sensational tabloid journalism in New York about electrocutions at Sing Sing prison which had made a violent impression on him. He recalled vividly the case of Ruth Snyder, one of the few women executed at the time, and he could remember the blurred but ominous photograph that had been sneaked of her in the electric chair and published on the front page of a newspaper. There had been a great deal of public revulsion against such executions during his formative years, and he had been affected by plays like Wexley's *The Last Mile* and Hollywood films with James Cagney walking through that little green door.

Second, Stan's mother had been a victim of tuberculosis, then a virtually incurable disease, and he had grown up from the age of four in the imminent expectation of her death. This, of course, had created a morbid atmosphere around the child and exaggerated the existential fear of death that is encountered in all of us. But many of us are exposed to the death and dying of close relatives and all of us of that generation were exposed to the same newspaper stories and films. Why did Stan fasten on the subject of death by electrocution? And why torment mice with electrical shocks? Stan's father had been an electrical contractor. His shop was fitted with a test bench that included a set of electrodes for checking the circuits of motors and other equipment. It was a favorite sport of the old-timers around the place, including Stan's father, to take hold of the electrodes in their bare hands and feel the tickle of current passing through their fingers. As a small boy, Stan had been encouraged, really bullied, into doing the same. Though eventually he became proud of his willingness to do this, he never entirely lost his fear.

Stan's father had gone further. In the shop or even at home when it was necessary to determine whether there was "juice" in a socket, the standard practice of the old pros was to stick a finger into the socket and feel for the current. The father had, on many occasions, challenged the boy to do the same. Somehow, this had been more frightening than touching the electrodes of the test bench. What was there about putting your finger into a socket (hole) and getting shocked that was especially alarming? When Stan, now an adult, considered the question, he was amused by the obvious sexual symbolism. The father challenged the boy to explore the female sex organ but at the risk of death by electrocution. Stan recalled only too clearly that there had been a ferocious competition between his father and himself for the mother's attention and love. Hostility had run high on both sides.

The dream seems to say, then, that the boy and, later, the man felt fear of electrocution (the method of choice) by his father as punishment for his special place in his mother's affections; that he carried with him an exaggerated fear of death in general because he grew up in a morbid atmosphere created by his mother's chronic and ultimately fatal illness. Further, the fact of the tuberculosis was kept a family secret. Even close family friends were given no hint of the true nature of the illness. Somehow, shame and embarrassment were associated with it. So, from early childhood, the boy had felt estranged from others by the heavy secret he was required to keep from everyone. Add it all up and Stan had very specific reasons to feel guilt toward his father, his mother, his friends and the world in general. And he had good reason to suspect that when he got his comeuppance it would be by way of electrocution!

Is Stan a special case? We are all special cases. That's why each of us has his unique dreams. This one dreams of electrified mice, adding machine murders, executions at Sing-Sing; others dream of ball games, fecal ropes, public figures with hermaphroditic appendages. But, too, we are all very much the same, conditioned by the same prevailing social values, social relations, socially determined culture, commerce and sexual taboos. Though our dreams are different, they usually deal with the same problem areas of guilt, inadequacy and alienation. Stan's immediate and pressing problem is alienation; he is troubled about his work. He feels he has an identity crisis, wanting the material rewards of commercial television but despising the character of the work demanded of him. He feels split down the middle and unable to function at anywhere near capacity. He is also, as we have seen, suffering from a problem of sexual identity that feeds neatly into this crisis. Does all this add up to an impossible tangle? Only if Stan expects a "cure" that will resolve all his problems and turn him into an insufferable paragon.

Short of that, he must accept the fact that, despite the handicaps of a rough childhood (like most of us) and that he lives in a confused and troubled world (like all of us), his own life demonstrates the considerable resilience and spirit of our kind because he has, indeed, been a very productive man. Alienation in work will not be overcome in any foreseeable future for most of us but it will be easier to live with if its sources are understood. Hopefully, too, an understanding of alienation will make it easier to do something about it. Meanwhile, the suffering of Stan's little white mice will have to be mitigated by the fact that they ride around so stylishly in that fine old Bentley.

Sex and Violence

Who peyntede the leoun, tel me who?
By God! if wommen had writers stories,
As clerkes han with-inne hir oratories
They wolde have writen of men more
wickednesse
Than all the mark of Adam may redresse.
· CHAUCER ·

ELEANOR

Undercover Girl

I am masquerading as a call girl but I'm really an undercover agent for the police. My task is to help catch two
gangsters. There is another call girl also working with the
police, and this woman is the girl friend of one of the two
wanted men. She has fixed me up with the other gangster.
I suddenly realize that this is occurring, of all places, just
three doors away from the apartment building in which I
lived with my mother during high school and where my
mother still lives. The other girl and I understand that we

are decoys. The police will raid as soon as the men arrive for the rendezvous. I am very excited; so is the other girl, and so are the police. We're all worried whether it will go off smoothly. I keep looking out the window, anxious and fearful. I have a change of clothing with me because I plan to go to my mother's place and get out of the floozy clothing after the action is over. But I don't want the police to know about the other clothes for fear they'll think I'm jeopardizing the project. We wait and wait; nothing happens, and I'm becoming bored and restless. Then, knowing I'm taking an unnecessary risk, I feel compelled to walk over to my mother's building. While I am en route, the gangsters arrive and encounter me. I dissemble, telling them that I'm going to drop something off at my mother's because she just happens to live nearby. I am terrified; perhaps they'll realize I am a policewoman. So I become very soothing, and they respond in a cozy way despite their aggressive New York style. Then the police arrive too soon, a whole carload of them. It's becoming more and more like a Keystone comedy except that it isn't funny. I am afraid for my life, trembling in terror. I experience a helpless fury toward myself, sure that I flubbed it by going to my mother's. Horror-stricken, I expect shooting and expect that the gangsters will hold me hostage. But my fears are unjustified. The police leap from their car with drawn handguns and the gangsters surrender immediately, offering no resistance.

Eleanor is in her early thirties, a poet and folk musician. She is very gifted and hardworking, but neurotic anxiety often results in stifling her creativity and she does experience oppressive feelings and fantasies of languishing away, single and lonely. Eleanor was an only child and she was about four years old when her father was killed in an accident. For reasons never fully clear to Eleanor, she was placed in foster homes during the rest of her childhood years while her mother earned a meager living. The mother reestablished a home when Eleanor was in mid-adolescence. During her early years, Eleanor felt like an abandoned child, an orphan.

When she was grown but still very young, she married a much older man who was quite wealthy. Their tacit arrangement was that she be like a child; he would care for all of her needs, but she must have no serious interests other than him. There were only rare sexual relations. As she entered her middle twenties, she began studying music seriously. It became clear that she could and would become a professional and thus move significantly toward adult autonomy. Her husband could not tolerate mature intimacy, sexuality and interdependence. He abruptly divorced her. Instead of recognizing this as her husband's problem, she assumed that the rupture of the marriage was evidence of her own inadequacy.

At the time of the above dream, Eleanor had begun a love relationship with a man who made no pretense of being an omnipotent and omniscient parent, who respected and encouraged her creative work and who did not indulge her tendency to see him as a father. Eleanor found this maturity refreshing but she recurrently expected her lover to leave her for another woman. She likens the sick part of herself to Marilyn Monroe who, we read, required Arthur Miller's constant attention and reassurance. This dependent tendency appears in the dream in her preoccupation with visiting her mother (returning to the childhood apartment in the midst of the frightening gangster caper); it also manifests itself when, in the dream, she casts herself as a call girl who depends for her survival on the favors of men. She identifies with the women in films and crime stories who move into prostitution and hapless dependency upon unscrupulous men who have skillfully fed their drug habit.

However, there is much more than dependency in the dream. There is terror and excitement; there is her role, not only as a call girl, but as a policewoman. Eleanor can recall frequent dreams of the Mafia, of being under the sway of a mysterious, lethal, criminal underground network. She is attracted to that kind of power, feeling both helpless and fascinated. It is very thrilling to be raped (in a

SEX AND VIOLENCE

dream) by a man who is so powerful and dangerous. Having lost her father at an early age, she has a strong disposition to seek in men the mythic, idealized, potent and sometimes ruthless dominator, the father who requires her self-subordination—and in exchange will "protect" her.

Through most of history, we have known only male-dominated cultures. Although changes are occurring with dizzying speed, the phallocentric trends are deeply ingrained in all of us—including Eleanor. For Eleanor and her many sisters who have experienced the cruel loss of a father—and his love—at an age when she could respond only with deep and inchoate emotions of sadness, resentment, guilt and eventual self-hatred, this cultural trend of male dominion converges with the special problems of these women to augment feelings of helplessness, inadequacy and resentment. So the sexual element in the manifest dream is also a vehicle (the car) carrying and displaying Eleanor's sustained preoccupation with power, dominance and submission. Eleanor is ambivalent in her attitude toward herself. She is depreciated, a call girl—but even this sexualized submission has a certain cunning power. And she is really an "officer of the law"—this is the real power she seeks; sanctioned, respectable and with the immense force of a whole society at her disposal.

Another important factor that enhances Eleanor's feelings of inadequacy is her strong unconscious identification with her mother. From the time of her father's death, Eleanor's mother was never able to reestablish a complete family life. We do not know what compelling reasons the mother may have had for making this choice, but Eleanor, as a child, certainly saw this as evidence of weakness and incompleteness on her mother's part. Eleanor's unconscious counterpart reaction was to limit her own sense of completeness—as a woman, as a person. Thus, she stayed within the same boundaries of fulfillment as her mother. This could be a paradigm of the cultural dilemma faced by all women today; consciously a woman wants to achieve equality, but her unconscious model of feminine identity is an archaic one based on her mother's life of psychological bondage. This conflict between conscious self-respect and unconscious self-degradation is multiplied by the hundreds of millions and becomes one of the powerful dynamic phenomena for humankind.

Eleanor's artistic creativity and her psychological integrity have enabled her to portray graphically in dream and fantasy the conflicts which have special importance for her. Such conflicts occur in virtually all women and are probably both psychological and biological in their origin. For example, in early adolescence, Eleanor had dreams and fantasies of being romantically kidnapped into a harem in, say, Baghdad, forced (to appease her guilt) by her handsome abductors into a sexual situation in which a series of men became increasingly direct in the sexual approach—the last one, to her immense satisfaction, culminating in the sex act. These are experimental sexual events for lively, imaginative young girls. Some extra violence probably persisted in Eleanor, as evidenced by her dreams of the Mafia and gangsters, and by slight residual stigmata in her present sex life—in that she (like many women) enjoys her lover's acting out rape-like behavior while he simultaneously withholds completion of the lovemaking.

There's a lot going on inside the emotional cauldron which is Eleanor, a fusion of cultural and biological factors, a mixture of slavery and unsuspected power, love and cruelty, caring and subjugating. This is a rich amalgam which promises a great deal of pleasure even if it doesn't offer any final explanations or any simplistic answers to the endlessly fascinating puzzle of the relationship between male and female, between man and woman.

There are changes occurring in today's world, changes that go to the very roots of many of our institutions. One might say that we are only now climbing painfully out of the period of man's prehistory, a period of scarcity when the great bulk of mankind had to struggle endlessly to produce the food and wherewithal for mere survival. We have learned to produce more food, more of everything with less effort, and we have also learned how to control the growth of population. We no longer really need to subordinate women, or anyone else. We can at last look forward to real equality for all. When that day comes, what will happen to the pattern of dominance-submission in which so many have found so much suffering and pleasure for so long? We don't know.

Perhaps at that poignant moment in human history, women, particularly gifted women, will assume a primacy in human affairs and lead us out of the existential wasteland spreading and growing around us. Men have suffered cruelly, women more so—for they have been deprived of freedom of choice which includes choosing between life and death. As women achieve their rightful share of power and freedom, their special suffering from the past may evolve into a unique wisdom—and save us all. It may be that this, too, is a latent message and promise in Eleanor's dream.

The
Alienation of Women

A man, though he be gray-haired can always get a wife,
But a woman's time is short.
· ARISTOPHANES ·

SUSAN

The Primal Scene

I am a child and I am entering my parents' bedroom. They
are naked under the covers and, as they see me enter, they
sit up in a startled way. They are furious with me but I
don't understand what I have done wrong. They denounce
me and tell me that they don't love me; and my mother
tells me that another reason for their rejection of me is that
she, my mother, has been a mental case. I just can't believe
or understand what has happened. I am crushed and in
despair.

Susan is in her thirties, unmarried, attractive, intelligent and with a fine education. She is extremely rigid and frustrated, especially in sexual matters. The oppressive commands of her conscience virtually immobilize her in any area of self-indulgence. Her few excursions into sex have given her pleasure but have terrified her and convinced her that she will be hopelessly besmirched if she permits herself to enjoy such contacts. This outrageous "conscience" was inspired by both of her religious parents, particularly her hysterical mother. Susan is terrified of sex because she fears the denunciation of the inner parental voices; so she leads an anguished single life, burning with sexual desire yet furious with friends who encourage a more relaxed, less moralistic attitude about sex.

Her dream goes right to the heart of the matter. Susan dares, in her dream, to exhibit sexual curiosity and interest about what her parents are up to naked in bed. For this she receives a lacerating denunciation. They tell her they don't love her, and the mother makes the horrifying revelation (not true) that she is or has been mentally unbalanced, thus cutting off even more finally any possible communication and feeling with the daughter. Susan is revealing to herself in the dream the source of her exaggerated and crippling conscience and the nature of the threat if she indulges herself sexually.

Susan's sexual conflicts and frustration have caused her to turn in on herself, have embittered her and alienated her in almost all her social contacts; so she dreams of the SLA, who deliberately set themselves into violent opposition to many of the organized institutions of society.

All the Way with the SLA

> I am a member of an SLA group. We are fugitives in danger of being killed. Then we are surrounded and are trying to figure out how to escape alive from the tall hotel we are in. We are both men and women in the group. Some sexual activity is going on. It feels as though a million FBI agents have surrounded us. I am very frightened.

Following this, there is a short secondary dream:

Ripped Off Anyway

> My automobile was in a parking structure just where it was
> supposed to be. But it has been ripped off. This parking
> place is near my own apartment. I feel extremely resentful
> about the loss of the car and I want to move away.

Susan, an only child, was convinced that her father had
really wanted a son. Her father was especially authoritar-
ian and she felt very close to her mother who died during
the girl's adolescence. This threw Susan and her father
into a greater intimacy, and the latent sexual feelings between the two came much closer to the surface though
neither ever expressed them.

The father began dating very young women, almost as
young as his daughter, and he would talk about his sexual
opportunities and exploits. This overstimulated Susan and
wounded her. She coped only moderately well with her
confused sexual feelings by working hard at school, re-
stricting herself to clean thoughts and no masturbation.
Subsequently, the father did settle into a marriage with a
woman more suitable than the nymphets with whom he
had been helling around. But Susan and her stepmother
became locked in a sexual rivalry for the father/husband.
Eventually Susan moved out of the situation and to another city.

Meanwhile, she completed her college studies and
graduate work. During those years, she had a series of sexless relationships with older men who were like understanding fathers. These were usually men upon whose
emotional support Susan could rely, who advised her and
who even encouraged her to take small steps toward more
overt sexuality. Her religious convictions waned, but she
became a special teacher in a Jewish parochial school.
Somewhere along the way, Susan became increasingly interested in liberal political causes.

Dating was a nightmare. Susan felt very much attracted

to men but she could not cope with their inevitable sexual advances. She refused to permit serious sexual activity because she continued to believe that sex outside of marriage was wrong, if not sinful, and would consign her to the hell of whoredom. By the age of twenty-eight, she was desperate, bit the bullet, had intercourse and liked it. But she arbitrarily decided that she could permit herself only two men before marriage because otherwise she would consider herself a whore. There was one love affair but the man was selfish and unwilling or unable to commit himself. She left him. As she moves into her thirties, Susan is increasingly frightened, frustrated and bitter. She feels that society, her personal history and her own values have conspired to force her to live in chronic sexual deprivation and with the prospect of barren spinsterhood.

Susan feels she has a right to be free and sexually gratified but the gratification available to her offends her harsh and scrupulous moral code. The SLA becomes a splendid symbol. She sees the group as suicidal, insane and terrifying. But she deeply envies their freedom to be aggressive and sexual. In effect, she feels that if you're going to be alienated from society, you may as well go all the way and have some fun out of it. But, always, she is terrified at harboring such thoughts. Look at the dream. Just for associating with the SLA, she is trapped by a "million" police agents who threaten her life. Of course, Susan recognizes how narrowly conventional are her attitudes and she deplores this side of herself. Furthermore, look where her nice moralistic conventions get her. Her succeeding dream says: she has a car in a parking structure near her apartment, all entirely proper . . . but it is ripped off anyway. The two dreams pair up to say that she is being crushed between two jaws: if she joins the SLA, she will enjoy a pathetically brief fling—and then the firing squad! If she remains her nice and proper self, abjures sex and violence, maintains a neat little apartment and a stall for her car, even this gratification (represented by the cherished car) will be taken from her, i.e., age alone will rob her of all opportunities for "proper" gratification.

Susan's dreams tell her that she feels trapped and thwarted by all these factors of her sexual inhibitions, the threat of spinsterhood, the social evaluation of herself and her conditions. She envies the SLA's "fuck you" attitude to society, would like to embrace it but cannot. She feels lost, without a place in our world; she fantasizes giving up her work and keeping on the move, constantly changing her locale so that there is never even an excuse to try to make connection.

Here, we have emphasized the psychological rather than the social factors giving rise to feelings of alienation, but it would be a serious error to think that this woman is suffering only from her personal, family and religious background. To see this in long perspective, we need only imagine that we have been describing a man rather than a woman. Would such a man, an attractive man approaching thirty, have occasion to feel so sexually pressured? Would he feel at this age that he was coming to the end of the line and must grab for sex and love or be forever deprived? Even with a strong religious background, it is unusual for a man with the kind of breadth, intelligence and liberality displayed by Susan, to suffer such severe sexual inhibitions today. And it would be quite rare for such an attractive young man to feel that he was rapidly outliving his value in the marriage market.

Society has declared that more than half our population must be alienated purely by virtue of sex. If workers feel alienated because their labor is appropriated, can we begin to appreciate how alienated women feel because their bodies have been appropriated for the sexual satisfaction of men? We refer here to the almost universal social assumptions toward sexual pleasure, attitudes so long in force and so widely accepted that the men and even the women affected are incapable of understanding what they feel.

Related to this question of sexual exploitation is the matter of the differential in the "aging" rate between men and women. Why is it assumed that in marriage and love the woman should be the younger partner? Only because she loses her child-bearing function at a certain age; for many millennia under primitive conditions, this was a vital factor. But this is no longer meaningful or it is meaningful in reverse. With today's population problems, it might be socially constructive if we reversed the situation and developed the attitude that women were more sexually attractive after menopause. Will that ever happen? We don't know. But we are convinced that if mankind survives long enough, the time will come when the present attitudes between men and women, based on primitive starvation-oriented societies, will change.

Despite her almost fanatic sexual repression, Susan has recently begun to permit herself some sexual gratification, at least in her dreams.

Me and the Beautiful Beach Boys

> I have gone for a vacation to a South Pacific island or I am teaching aborigines in a mission school—it is not clear. Also, the setting keeps shifting from a rather messy and disorderly village to a lush grove of coconut palms shading a beautiful white sand beach in a lagoon. Suddenly, a group of powerful Polynesian men spring on me. They all rape me. Naturally, I am outraged but I'm having a ball. They're all like beautiful beach boys. I'm carried away by fused images of dazzling white teeth, broad smiles and deep voices, velvety bronze skin flecked with cool drops of seawater and firm rippling muscles underneath. I am able to reach orgasm with one of the men. I fall in love with him; we marry; we have a baby and we live happily and simply in a local village. Toward the end, a dark, sad feeling pervades the dream; it's all painful and vague now. I am on a boat returning to the U.S.A. I have lost my lover forever.

For Susan, with her enormous sexual guilt and frustration, such a rape dream is just what the safety engineer ordered, a good escape valve. It is basically nonviolent;

she is abducted by a group of very horny men who do her no harm. Initially, she resists; then she reaches orgasm and, finally, becomes very cooperative with the men in their lusty enterprise. The initial resistance appeases her guilt so that she can go on to enjoy the sexual fun. But, sadly, Susan has not overcome or really fooled her implacable sexual conscience. She has only lulled it for a few moments during sleep and thus stolen a bit of fantasy pleasure, not actual sexual fulfillment. It remains true that she rarely has a date and hasn't had sex for over a year. Like so many, she is the victim, not the mistress of her sexual conscience. And even in her "happy" dream, she eventually succumbs to a feeling of sorrow and futility.

On the same night as this rape dream, Susan had another dream:

Father and the Bride

> I am in Southern California where I meet a young man from a wealthy Sacramento family (Susan is from Sacramento). His name is Clum. He is wearing a coat and his pockets are filled with thin books, all about his family. He uses these books somehow to con women, and thus he can get away from his family. Clum is a nice guy. Then he and I are married; there is a beautiful view of a bay from our home, and I can hardly believe I've finally really made it. Now we are in bed but, strangely, I'm unresponsive. Clum leaps out of bed and asks my father what kind of foreplay would work on me. Dad implies that he knows how to turn me on but it would scarcely be right for him to demonstrate. Clum keeps pleading and, finally, my father softens his position. He asks if I'm asleep; I say, "No, I'm not." Then Clum and I are making love. It's tremendously exciting and I have a terrific orgasm.

Who is Clum? Who is this clumsy, inept but amiable lover who cannot make her come until Dad shows him how? Is he another mask for Dad? A distilled, denatured, unthreatening surrogate whom Susan can permit herself to marry and make love to without the awful menace of the incest taboos? Probably. After all, he did carry around those pockets full of thin books through which "he can get away from his family." We don't know what the thin books are but if Clum (father) can use any means to get away from his family, then (as a man without a family) it should be all right for him to marry Susan. Of course, Clum is one of those portmanteau dream figures that represent many things. He can be Susan's father; he can also be Susan herself in a different guise. But we are hot in pursuit of Susan's priority problem: her sexualized relationship with her father. If this dream spells out that aspect of her problem so clearly, what light does it shed on her rape dream?

Interestingly, her rape dream is not truly menacing, not the brutal assault of a single man. It is relatively benign and takes the form of gang fucking. Why the gang? It would appear that this is an effective way for Susan to depersonalize her incestuous wish; even in her dream she cannot be accused of sleeping with an individual who might be her father when, in fact, she is sleeping with a whole flock of attackers. Were she to individualize her dream rapist, she might more quickly have to recognize the true identity of the sexual assailant of her dreams. But it was not until the second dream, above, the dream of "Clum" that she ever encountered her father directly in any of her sex dreams. Only now must Susan face the source of her sexual guilt and, hopefully, come to terms with it.

For Susan, then, her dream of rape helped by giving her a bit of sexual gratification and release but, also, it was a red herring serving to mislead her, to cover up the trail, to disguise the true direction of her sexual drive. The rape dream helped Susan to live with herself because it enabled her to deny the identity of her dream lover (and Susan had many such rape dreams with the same pattern). For a long while, for most of her life, it would have been too painful and threatening for her to face her forbidden incestuous wishes, a circumstance which reinforced all the other religious and personal factors and aggravated to the extreme her sexual inhibitions.

Now, she is more mature, stronger, hungrier to tackle her problems without self-deceit; so at last she permits herself the dream of Clum in which her father enters the sexual arena quite openly. This dream dramatically expresses for her the central truth about her sexualized relationship with her father, a truth she has been ducking for almost twenty years. Now she knows on what battlefield her war of sexual liberation must be waged. After this forthright dream, she can admit to herself her repressed wish from childhood that her father make love to her. She can begin to unburden herself of her enormous sexual guilt.

Susan will continue to live in a world where sexual alienation is the rule for women and guilt hovers over every sexual encounter, but she is also part of a world where change is occuring with unprecedented speed. Through her dreams, she can now begin to understand herself better and understand the roots of her problems; she can also understand that she shares most of her problems with most of the women she is likely to meet, even those who didn't.have a religious upbringing, a mother who died too young, a father who was seductive and punitive. What a relief to know she does not have to feel alienated from all those other women!

IV

THE
ART
of the
SEXUAL DREAM

.

Dreams are the true interpretation of our inclinations
but there is art required to sort and understand them.
· MONTAIGNE ·

The dream is the royal road to the unconscious.
· FREUD ·

We have presented over fifty dreams, the profiles of the dreamers and dream analyses in varying degrees of depth in order to convey the concept that dreams are the arena where individuals may, if they wish, confront the deepest truths about themselves.

We have focused almost exclusively on the overtly sexual dream and have shown its great versatility and constancy in the mirroring of the dreamer's sexual, interpersonal and psychosocial dimensions.

Now, we will attempt to explain the "art of the dream" in a somewhat more formal, systematic and, at times, mechanistic way. There is no intention to make analysts or self-analysts of the readers. But we hope that every reader's psychological life will be enriched by a greater understanding of his own dreams.

If it is understood that dreams are not commodities, not mere by-products of the mind, that the dream is part of the dreamer and the dreamer is present in every part of his dream; if it is understood that dreams are the "royal road to the unconscious," we can move on to the "art that is required to sort and understand them."

As in any art, the most compelling element is the drive of the artist, not the mechanics of the craft. It is not learning to mix colors, studying to embroider phrases or practicing the rules of musical construction that separate the artist from the dilettante; it is the genuine hunger to create and communicate. So, with dreams, we must have a hunger to understand ourselves better, a need for personal growth, a desire to relate more meaningfully to all whose lives we touch in our family, work, community, world. Only then can we begin to make important use of our dreams; otherwise we only learn some amusing parlor tricks.

If you understand that the dream *is* you; if you have a genuine need for self-knowledge, you are ready to walk through the looking-glass (it is a looking-glass) into the world of dreams. But before we spell out the topsy-turvy roles of this "Wonderland" where the White Rabbit, the Mad Hatter, the Dormouse and the March Hare all have a great deal to say, it would be well to recall again that dreams are your ultimately personal possession. The only value they have is to you. There is no need to get into a numbers game about your dreams. In our consumer society, the dreamer may tend to feel successful and proud if he is a frequent and copious dreamer. This will show that he is winning the big dream competition and that he is well on the way to becoming a dream millionaire. (One recent author reports with pride of having recorded over ten thousand dreams.) A single dream thoughtfully explored can be a much more productive source of self-understanding than dozens of dreams superficially or self-deceptively interpreted. It is not unusual for a single dream which occurred years before to be a continuing source of revelation as it is examined, reviewed and reinterpreted in the light of maturer understanding. Or, a dream recalled from childhood may become very significant when it is finally studied and understood by the adult.

This can become a voyage of discovery into what is for most of us (how could it be otherwise?) the most fascinating *terra incognita* of all.

HELPING YOU REMEMBER YOUR DREAMS

Many people have trouble recalling their dreams. Some are convinced they never dream. Current clinical information confirms that everyone dreams repeatedly through the night. "Not dreaming" is only forgetting or repressing the dream. To help you recall your dreams, here are a few pointers.

1. The ability to recall dreams is strongly influenced by your interest in them, by your desire to recall them. If, as a result of reading about dreams, you become interested in your own, you will automatically start to become more aware of them, start to remember fragments at least; and soon you may have more dreams to study than you can cope with.

2. Since dreams tend to fade with extreme rapidity, it is essential to hang tight to the initial recall on awakening. Then, to fix the dream in your conscious mind, you should mentally put it into words as though you are telling it to someone. The act of converting the dream into words is what brings it fully into the arena of consciousness and permits it to be imprinted on that area of memory which can be readily recalled. Most of us are familiar with a dream or two which we had long ago, spoke about and then could recall clearly over the years.

3. To help in your understanding and later recall of

dreams, it is useful when reviewing your dreams in the morning to jot down some quick associations to the dream.

CHECKLIST FOR DREAMERS

Apart from the specific suggestions that follow, it should be emphasized that all dreams must be considered in relation to the entire history of the dreamer. Every dream must be viewed in terms of both the current circumstances and the early life and special conditions that helped to shape the personality.

The current circumstances will include whatever is happening in the dreamer's life at the time of the dream, whether happy or unhappy. Is this a productive and satisfying epoch for the dreamer? Is he enjoying a good marriage, a stimulating love affair, success in his work? Or is this a time of painful crisis, or mourning, divorce or financial reverse? Such factors will be reflected in the dream. Similarly, the unique personal memories from the dreamer's developmental years, whether the experiences were productive or traumatic, continue to play a powerful role throughout his psychological life and, therefore, in his dreams. These memories of the past, too, may range from one pole to the other, from the remarkably satisfied childhood of a boy or girl who was well loved, who was a prodigious scholar or an admired athlete —to the harsh trauma of having been the son or daughter of a child-battering parent. In all likelihood, the past of any individual includes events both happy and unhappy and the entire spectrum in between. All will be found in his dreams.

1. Free Association

Despite the controversies that continue to roil around him, Freud was certainly the father of modern dream interpretation. When he employed dreams in the therapeutic situation between patient and analyst, he developed the use of free association as the key to unlocking the content of the dream. In free association the patient tries to say, without constraint or censorship, whatever comes into his mind while recalling the dream. For example, we related the case of George, a man who dreams he is being sodomized by his father. After such a dream, George might have associated as follows:

"I can't be certain how I felt about what was happening in the dream, whether I was frightened or whether I struggled. That part isn't at all clear. I know that, actually, I was always a little afraid of my father. I never felt he loved me as much as my mother did. I can remember the day of my mother's funeral. I was thirteen years old. I had been weeping at the cemetery and I saw my father weep for the first and the last time. Even though I felt grief-stricken and bereft at seeing my mother lowered into the grave, I can recall reacting with surprise to my father's tears.

"That night when I went to bed at home, I was frightened and felt very much alone. My father finally came up to my bedroom, which is something I never remember his doing before. He didn't have anything much to say, just patted my head. I held back my tears because his eyes were dry by now. I wanted him to stay; I wished he would sleep in the bed and not leave me all alone but I knew I was too old for that kind of thing and I never suggested it to him. After a while he just pulled the covers up to my chin, say good-night and went away. I lay there for a long time wondering how I would get along now that my mother was gone. It seemed like a long time until I realized that I was lying there with an erection. I was horrified that I should feel like masturbating at a time like this. I told myself I wouldn't do it; that if I did I would die or something else terrible would happen to me. I told myself that if my father came in and caught me jerking off at a time like this he would kill me. But it seemed my penis got harder and harder; it wouldn't go away. I couldn't get to sleep, and so I started to rationalize about how it wouldn't do any harm and I had to get to sleep. Finally, I went ahead and I enjoyed it more than usual. Afterwards, I felt very guilty. I no longer believed in God; I didn't think my mother was up in heaven watching me but I surely felt uneasy; I felt that in some magical or mysterious way I would sooner or later pay for this foul behavior.

"Nevertheless, I was more relaxed. I became drowsy and I had many free-floating thoughts. I can't recall them now but I know they weren't so much about my mother as you would expect. They were more about the future and how it was going to be between me and my father. I suppose I was anxious about the next act.

"Looking back over those years I feel, for the first time, puzzled about the strains between my father and myself. I always seem to recall the bad times between us but I know there were good times like when I'd go down to the packing plant with him very early on Saturday morning, and we'd have steaming mugs of coffee and sweet rolls; I was treated as one of the guys around the plant, and I admired my father because he was the boss and everyone seemed to look up to him. I can remember the winter dark outside, the glaring unshaded bulbs in the huge walk in refrigerators with the yellow sides of beef hanging on racks, the constant cold that always got me first in the toes and the muted smell of the cold meat that would follow you anywhere in the building, even in the hallways, even in the offices with their old oak desks and their little round electric heaters where you warmed your hands and feet. I think I must have loved my father a lot at times like that or I wouldn't remember it all so well, but I never seem to recall any of the good feelings between us—not until today."

The dreamer seems to be working his way toward understanding his early and protracted need for a loving relationship with his father, something which the dream dramatizes in a startling fashion. Perhaps such a violent metaphor for love was the only way to drill through the many decades of denial which had silted over the original feelings, the only way to force the dreamer to reexamine his feelings for his father.

When you tackle your own dreams, let your thinking range freely; let it take you wherever it will without fear, constraint or censorship. Don't try to force anything. But see what memories, what thoughts come up to associate with your dream. Only later, when you are through with this exercise, try to see what links have emerged between the dream and the waking thoughts stirred up by it. As in the above example, you may find yourself recalling events you think you have long forgotten. You may savor again the crumpets and tea or coffee and sweet rolls of long ago. You may uncover feelings for others buried so deeply that it is as if they never existed—until now when you rediscover them.

2. Study the Manifest Content

By manifest content we mean simply the literal story of the dream without any attempt to study it for symbols or deeper meanings. If you dream, like Susan, that you are watching your parents naked under the covers and they start to scream at you; like Mark, that you are in a charnel house sucking on a penis that resembles a brass faucet; like Phyllis, that you are in a fancy bordello; like Stan, that you are in the death house at Sing Sing prison; like Nancy, that a real estate broker is showing you a house with railroad tracks that run right through the middle . . . all these are the manifest content of the dream. And even this raw manifest content contains many clues to the meaning of the dream. For example, there was George who dreamed of a sexual encounter with his stepdaughter. This is a real stepdaughter; the sexual feelings are real. It is not necessary to go beyond this manifest content to learn something of value from the dream. At the very least, George, having no desire to become involved in such a messy situation, would be forewarned not to permit himself, unconsciously, to become seductive nor get himself into a situation like staying overnight in the girl's apartment. As we demonstrated when we analyzed this dream earlier, it is possible and desirable to go much further in interpreting the roots and meaning of such a dream but, for a start, even examining it on the level of its manifest content can be most useful.

If you have a vivid dream that seems merely to replay commonplace characters and events from your current life, it is safe to assume that the dream has a meaning beyond the mere repetition of the daily round. If, like Michael, you dream that you are enjoying *Playboy* and beating off but your ejaculation is not very thrilling (which is exactly what happened before you went to sleep), try to discover other facets of the dream—like your feeling, at age thirty, of shame that your distant parents may catch you in the act. (You didn't think about that when you were awake! Your waking mind was too sophisticated.) Use that as a place to dig in. The manifest content of a dream like this can be the starting point for a serious exploration of your sexual guilt.

Remember, though, that the manifest content functions to conceal, as well as reveal, the true meaning of your dream. The incestuous wishes of the man for his stepdaughter are only part of the truth, a part that the dreamer finds not too difficult to face. The latent portion, much less easy to accept, is the dreamer's long "forgotten" sexual drives toward both his mother and his father. The feeling for the stepdaughter, the manifest content, tends to screen the deeper meaning. And it is only with the deeper meaning that we gain the insight about our character formation, the knowledge with which we can change ourselves.

Another example of this is Michael's dream of watching the closed-circuit television exhibition of a sporting event. He couldn't see the screen. The whole dream was precipitated by a similar actual occurrence and might have been dismissed as mere replay of an annoying event from the man's daily life. But the events in the dream represented and screened the true subject matter, the dreamer's feelings about his parents' sexual intimacy when they were together in their bedroom and he, as a child, was excluded by a closed door.

The manifest content of the dream must be examined both for what it says and for what it conceals.

3. Look for Visual and Verbal Clues

It is the nature of dreams to use concrete visual symbols to express complex feelings and ideas. There is little use of sound or language in dreams. To use another analogy, when you dream, you are like a painter who must restrict himself to forms, colors, images to express everything he feels. This will involve you in some very abstract, impressionistic and tricky combinations. You may have to be quick to unravel the complex symbolism of your own dream. For example, a woman (Anne) dreamed that she was dancing at the U.S.O. (These letters stand for the United Service Organizations, a World War II serviceman's social organization where coffee, doughnuts, music and other harmless entertainment were offered to the soldiers and sailors by volunteer hostesses.) In her dream, Anne was having a wonderful time at the U.S.O. But she had never been to one, and this was years after the war. She woke and was puzzled about the pleasant dream until she pronounced the letters as though they were a word, i.e., U.S.O. became Uso. Then, she understood. She had recently met and dated a man named Usseau, which sounds exactly the same as Uso, and her dream told her she was falling in love with him. Verbal and visual puns are extremely common and frequently give the best clue to the meaning of your dream. A cock (male bird) may appear in the dream and represent a cock (penis); or "bird" or "chick" may appear and represent girl. Flowers, fields of grain, seeds may represent fertility and the wish of a woman for conception—or the fear of it. There is the host of commonplace symbols which are generally accepted: sharp, long or pointed objects like knives may stand for a phallus; so may a gun that shoots. Bags, purses, boxes may be symbols for the vagina. But it is not necessary to accept such symbols as unvarying. Try them on. See if the shoe fits. Only you can know if the symbol and the interpretation feel true. It's your scenario.

4. Relate the Dream to Present Events

After studying the dream for obvious manifest content and symbols, try relating the dream to anything that may have happened to you recently. This is what Freud described as the "day residue" that appears in dreams. A man named Leo dreams that he is riding a motorcycle. As he tries to park it, moving it backward very slowly and only inches at a time, a Negro seems to thrust his foot forward and grazes the tire with his shoe. But the contact is minimal. Leo is surprised to find the Negro very hostile. He claims he is seriously injured and wants to call the police. Though Leo is not worried by the threat of the police since he feels he has done nothing criminal, he is disturbed by the venom of the black man. After all, the whole episode has been trivial. But, now, the black man displays his leg which is covered with ugly bruises and burns such as might result from very heavy contact with a revolving tire. Leo is astonished and wonders how so much injury could have come about.

Waking, Leo puzzles about the dream. He does not own a motorcycle, has never driven one; he has no present contact with black people. But he associates to the dream and suddenly recalls that he was driving his car the day before and was in a great hurry. He was forced to wait at a pedestrian crosswalk while a Negro, with no show of haste, walked across the street. At the time, Leo had fleetingly thought that there were times and places where a Negro would not so casually delay a white man in an important-looking car.

Evidently the very minor and forgotten episode had

evoked feelings of hostility and guilt in the dreamer. The dream says that though Leo's "ideas" about black-white relations are exceedingly correct and up to date, deep in his heart he still harbors unacceptable feelings of hostility (he does injure the black man in the dream) and, also, a nagging sense of guilt (the injury to the black man was much worse than the dreamer had supposed or could explain). Such a dream and its interpretation help to bring into the light the deeply repressed feelings that must be examined and dealt with rationally if they are to be changed. Such a dream may also be studied for a deeper level of meaning beyond its manifest content. (See this same dream under "Latent Sexual Content.")

5. Identify Your Cast of Characters

Do you recognize yourself and the role you are playing in the dream? This is usually not difficult except that your unconscious likes to play the little trick of casting you simultaneously in more than one role. This is something you must learn to spot. For example, there is Simon who dreams of the great cat that is eating the flayed bunny alive. He is both the bunny and the cat; as the bunny he is the victim of the voracious mother (the cat) and he is also the devouring cat since he has adopted some of his mother's characteristics. There is Greg whose two children are being baked for eating; the children are also himself in this cannibalistic dream of self-hatred. There is Stan who, with his thinning hair, cannot boost his ladylove through the window while his efforts are observed by the very young man with the thick shock of dark hair; the young man in the dream is also Stan at an earlier age. There is Ella in a loft with her attorney where she finds and makes love to a little girl waif. Ella is also the unloved little girl.

Is there an authority figure in the dream? Is there a boss, a teacher, a doctor, lawyer or priest? What is your attitude toward the authority figure in the dream? Whatever patterns toward authority seemed to work for us in early childhood are likely to be carried through all our lives. By discovering such patterns and attitudes in our dreams we may learn to respond appropriately in the present moment to the present situation instead of carrying around forever the burden of the past.

If you can find an authority figure, can he or she be both a current one and one from the past like a parent? Can you see a connection through this from the early past to your present behavior? Laura's "boss" takes her to a motel and forces her to say "I want you to fuck me." It is not too difficult for Laura to recognize the incestuous wish thinly veiled in this dream and start to think through her confused feelings for her father. Michael is starting to have intercourse with a current girl friend when she draws away because it would be "incest." If Michael has any doubts about the meaning of this dream, he goes on to dream that he leaves to visit his father but finds him dead. The girl in the dream who is laying down the law about sex is clearly Michael's mother, and the roots of Michael's sexual problems begin to be exposed.

Siblings frequently appear in dreams either manifestly or in disguised form. When a child grows up with brothers and sisters he early establishes patterns of relating to them that will last throughout his life and influence how he relates to other people as an adult. He must compete with siblings for the attention and affection of parents; he must depend on them for love and support when attacked in the schoolyard; he may be the favored child, envied by the others, or the ugly duckling, or the Cinderella. From the infinity of situations that occur while growing up with sisters and brothers, including very important sexual encounters, the child learns many of life's lessons and develops attitudes with which to face the world. All this will certainly appear in his dreams.

From John's dream of undertaking to murder his two sisters in the hotel room, we learn that even as an adult he is still struggling to resolve strong feelings from childhood: his guilt over incestuous desires toward his sisters and his image of a shabby unromantic family life which they continue to personify. All this leads him back through the family constellation to a deeper understanding of his feelings for his father and a sharper appreciation of his own unrealistic behavior when, as an adult and light years away from his family background, he continues to act and feel as though he were still part of that family.

When Ella dreams of making love to a little girl in the studio loft, she is making love to herself, casting herself in the role of the abused waif who can't "come"; she is also recapitulating the childhood experience when she was virtually raped by an older sister and propositioned by still another sister. These experiences with her sisters, which she relives in her dreams, are basic to the problem of feminine identity which Ella struggles with as an adult.

Who are the other characters? If they are recognizable people, they may indeed be playing themselves in your dream, or they may be substituting for another person or for an abstract quality that cannot otherwise be represented in the dream. Patty Hearst, in the dreams we report, is actually unknown to the dreamers. She is a symbol of violence, freedom, license, social protest, a vehicle for whatever role the dreamer needs to clothe her with. In Ella's dream, Henry Kissinger appears as a powerful male figure but one who must be mocked and emasculated. Movie stars and other prominent personalities who impinge on our consciousness from the media frequently appear in our dreams. So do our accountants. Simon's plane is being piloted to a forced landing by his accountant in a piece of obvious symbolism. Blacks appear in our dreams as symbols of lubriciousness (Greg) or as victims (Leo). Study the interaction between yourself (the dreamer) and the other characters. Ask yourself why you invent the other characters or choose to people your dream play with them. No one is there without a reason.

6. Is There Any Overt Sexual Behavior in Your Dream?

We have emphasized dreams with overt sexual behavior because such dreams tell us most clearly what we need to know about our waking sex lives and also because such dreams, in our experience, are the most direct bridge to behavior in all other areas. In overt sex dreams we can observe ourselves in action. Are we sexually aggressive or repressed? Are we dominating or submissive? Are we gay (either way) or guilty? Do we enjoy being raped or fear it? Do we people our sex dreams with beautiful men and women or turn them into freaks? Is the sex gratifying or alarming? We have presented examples of all these reactions as encountered in dreams. We have seen how these sex-dream attitudes can be carried out of the bedroom or charnel house and illuminate all corners of our daily lives. When Ella dreams of men with teats, with deformed penises, with umbrella appendages that resemble vaginas, she is telling us more than how she feels about men in bed; she is revealing how she feels about men in life. When John leaves the "celebrated beauty" of his dream sexually unsatisfied, he is disclosing more than a problem of premature ejaculation; he is making an observation and comment about his feeling of lack of effectiveness and accomplishment in his professional life. When Phyllis dreams of going into an elegant brothel with a man, she is struggling not just for a more fulfilling sex life but for a more fulfilling life, a more satisfying identity as a woman—as a person.

7. Is There Latent Sexual Content?

Given the centrality of sex, sexual repression and guilt you can be virtually certain that there is a sexual component in any dream. Even the relatively "simple" dream of the man on the motorcycle encountering a black will yield important data on the dreamer's feelings of sexual guilt and inadequacy if pursued far enough. After all, the man is being held responsible for something he didn't really do; he is being threatened by a potent (black) male figure for injuring the leg (penis) though the dreamer's phallic symbol (motorcycle) was not involved in any serious contact with anything more than a shoe (vagina). Still, the dreamer has an uneasy feeling of guilt for having damaged the phallus of the potent male. All this is an obvious paradigm of the situation of the boy child caught between a seductive mother and a resentful father, a circumstance that was particularly true in the case of this dreamer.

But it is not usually necessary to look so far for the hidden sexual meaning. The man cutting off the head of a snake after dreaming of a tabooed relationship with his stepdaughter is one of the most obvious cases of sexual symbolism where snake equals penis. When Susan is with the SLA and they are surrounded in their hotel and almost captured by the FBI, there is only a passing reference to sexual activity, nothing clearly defined. Yet in the dream, Susan is surely working out her terrible feelings of sexual frustration in this male-centered world which condemns her (in her own eyes) to a life either as a whore or as a sexless old maid. Eleanor, too, in her dreams of playing cops and robbers with the frightening gangsters, is indulging in wishful dreams of violent and exciting sexual encounters which she thinly disguises by casting herself in the role of a peace officer. Most dreams, if studied carefully, will disclose some underlying sexual wish or attitude.

8. Does the Locale of the Dream Mean Anything to You?

Do you dream of being in a church though you haven't been in one for years? Do you dream of the place you work, your school, your home? Do you dream of a charnel house? Does your behavior in life seem appropriate to such a background? How can you relate the place to your feelings and problems? Are you, like Phyllis, a respectable middle-class woman, who finds herself in her dreams wandering through a whorehouse district? Phyllis is struggling to shake off the pallid conventionality of her sex life; her dreams, thrusting her into the brutal, frightening but beckoning ambience of the prostitute, make certain she doesn't miss the point. Susan, in her dream, chooses to be raped on the romantic beach of a South Sea island. It's quite clear from this choice of locale that Susan hungers for such an experience, welcomes it. She's not mucking up her rape scene with dark and sinister figures who attack her in the prosaic confines of her own bedroom. The setting of your dream play is as significant as the setting of any real play.

9. What Is the Feeling of Your Dream?

It is most important to identify the dominant emotion of the dream. Were you feeling happy, sad, angry, terrified, eager, hopeless? From the feeling we get the best clue to the meaning and the best check on whether the interpretation is right for you. Dreams, above all, are about feeling. When Arnie, who has been lusting for Yvonne for quite some time, finally has her in the bar in his dream, he is not happy and fulfilled; he is confused and anxious; he is not handily achieving his sexual goal; rather, he is struggling with his fears about impotence, his hostility toward women, his anxiety about competing with other men, his confusion of sexual identity. Whereas Susan, raped on the South Seas beach is having quite a good time. Each must look to the feeling of the dream as a starting point for understanding its content.

10. Consider Your Dreams in Series

Several dreams in a single night are apt to be related. They are probably triggered by the same life problem that is preoccupying you at the moment. If you recall such a series of dreams, it is usually easier to extract their essential meaning because the different dreams will represent several different angles of attack on the same trouble spot. Thus, Ella dreams in the same night that 1) she is dancing with Henry Kissinger, who is built like a hermaphrodite; 2) that she is having marvelous sexual fun with a man whose penis turns out to be monstrously malformed and

3) that she notices another man on the street who has, in addition to a penis, an umbrella-like appendage that resembles a vagina. There can be little doubt with so much reinforcement that Ella is working out her hostility for men, caricaturing them and deforming them to equalize the situation. There is Stan who has two dreams that appear unrelated. The first deals with the problem of wiring and tormenting white mice; the second is the search for a murderer via adding-machine tape. If there is any question of the alienation theme of the first dream, the second dream, which focuses so sharply on "murder equals business," makes it quite clear that Stan, whatever his other problems, is trying to resolve a moral and existential dilemma about his social role.

11. Wishes

If there is one thing that we all seem to have heard about dream interpretation, it is that dreams represent wishes. But our dreams certainly don't seem to gratify our wishes—for a new car, a new house, a job, career or romance for which we may yearn. Most of the dreams we have reported are full of tension, anxiety and even terror. How, then, do they represent wish fulfillment?

Stekel, one of the early psychoanalysts, put it this way: "The dream expresses a search for deliverance from the life conflict or from the present-day conflict." In this deeper sense, then, the dream is a wish, a wish to resolve the problems that plague us in our waking life. A woman may dream repeatedly of being assaulted, raped, murdered. In her dreams, she carefully sets the stage of a world that is violent and menacing; she peoples that stage with brutal men who assault her mercilessly. Since she is the creator of the dream, the playwright, the set designer, we ask ourselves what wishes are served by these frightening dream experiences to which she unconsciously chooses to subject herself. Partly, no doubt, as with any audience that enjoys horror films, she benefits from the catharsis, the opportunity to live out her worst fears in a world of fantasy (dream or film) where she may experience the feelings of terror without being exposed to the physical reality. At the end of the dream, as at the end of a film, she can get up, uninjured, and go her way.

But there is a deeper, more constructive function for her dreams. After all, she is placing *herself* on the stage; she is trying to *interact* with the frightening characters of her psychodrama. True, she sees herself as victim, but *not only as victim*. She is making a "search for deliverance from the life conflict"; and eventually she invents a dream where she is hurting herself, where she becomes the victim of her own self-inflicted pain.

Thus, a woman who is convinced that she is not loved, that she cannot be loved, may discover in her dreams that she is creating her own world of pain, that it is not simply imposed on her by others. Her dreams are offering to fulfill her deepest wish, offering to deliver her, with the truth, from her irrational conviction that she can expect only pain in her relationships with others.

There is a wish even in a nightmare, a wish for understanding, for deliverance, for resolution of conflict. Understood this way, we will find a "wish" in every dream. And we must look for that wish because, when we find it in our dream, we will have identified the area of conflict that troubles us.

Let's examine a few dreams "by the numbers" to demonstrate how it may be done.

DAN'S TWO DREAMS

Dan has two dreams that are not related in time. The dreams are totally different. One has no overt sexual content; the other has nothing but. Dan was asked to tell his dreams and discuss them with the help of the guidelines proposed in this section. The two dreams lead into different areas of free association but, despite the gross disparities, Dan comes back to a consideration of the same problems that trouble him. The dreams are accurately recorded and the dreamer, of course, is real. Dan's discussion is presented faithfully except for such changes as are necessary to protect privacy. We offer these as examples of how others may begin to study their own dreams for the purpose of better self-understanding.

PERSONAL BACKGROUND:

Dan is in his mid-forties. He is a professor in a science department of a major public university. He has been married to the same wife for almost twenty years; there are four children, and the marriage appears to be stable. But there are problems, especially in relation to sex. Dan complains that his wife is grudging about sex, that she invariably climbs into bed with a heavy sigh and a remark about how tired she is. This he reads as a signal that she doesn't want to make love, and it infuriates him. Each time, in order to make love, he must guiltily impose on his wife's fatigue so that he may take his pleasure. He finds this demeaning. Sometimes he will go for weeks without trying to make love to her, waiting to see if she will just once get into bed without her inevitable litany, if she will, once, snuggle up beside him, initiate sex play. But, of course, while this waiting game proceeds, a terrible tension builds between husband and wife, thus making sex more and more difficult. The wife appears not to notice the tension until it gets out of hand and explodes in an angry argument. (This, of course, is Dan's version. The wife would tell it quite differently.)

In a sense, it is surprising that Dan cares this much about sex since, when he manages to get beyond the above-described game, it isn't all that great. Sex is initiated with resentment and fraught with anxiety. Although he almost invariably brings his wife to climax, he seldom manages a really satisfying ejaculation.

Dan is not trained in psychology and he has never been psychoanalyzed. Like most educated people today, he has read books on psychology and he has picked up some of the language and concepts, as will be evident in his remarks. He probably functions in this area on about the same level as the well-informed layman who may read this material and try to use it for greater self-understanding.

One point merits emphasis because it intrudes into the dream discussion. Having read our introductory material and having carefully studied the preceding "Checklist for Dreamers," Dan's thinking and feeling were directly influenced by this circumstance; he began to recall his dreams more clearly; his dreaming was probably prejudiced by his participation in our informal project; and, of necessity, he assumed a relationship with the doctor with whom he had contact through this experiment. Though never a patient of the doctor, Dan also assumed some of the privileges of the patient, i.e., the right to unload his emotional problems on the doctor. Therefore, the doctor may appear in the dream and in the discussion.

Of course, there is an additional difference between Dan and another individual who may read this book and use it for self-understanding. Dan related his dreams to the authors, worked with them and was encouraged to elaborate his discussion. He was inevitably influenced by this interplay. Accordingly, his consideration of his own dreams is more sophisticated than one would expect. But we offer the following as a demonstration of what one bright dreamer might extract from a serious study of his own dreams.

THE DREAM:

I am in a shop; it feels like a foreign country. The shop sells all sorts of things: curios, sundries, souvenirs. It may also be a café. I am particularly looking for some tobacco. I don't want the large blue tin or the very small package but rather the medium-size blue-paper package, like the Edgeworth used to come in. There is a friend with me; I can't identify him. A woman is in charge of the shop and no one else is there at first. After a great deal of searching, we find just the package I want. I also pick up a bottle of booze and a third purchase which I can't now recall. But there definitely were three. I give the woman a twenty-dollar bill and begin to wonder if I will get change since we have not discussed the price of anything. But I feel certain that I am entitled to some change. We wait. Meanwhile, other people have appeared and seem to be lined up at the checkout register presided over by the same woman. It is rather like the cashier's desk at a busy café just as the lunch crowd is leaving. Since the woman pays no attention to me, I want to call her attention to the fact that I am waiting for my change. I am reluctant to make a public issue of it. What if she has been trying to cheat me and I expose her this way? I do finally remind her that I am waiting for change. She seems embarrassed and worried by this. The new situation causes a delay, and the people in line are impatient. Some attack her for apparently trying to cheat me; others are inclined to attack me because I am so vague about what to do and seem more concerned about how I may have damaged the woman that I am about my but I have no proof of this. Perhaps she only works there and what I have done will cost her her job. I am in doubt about what to do and seem more concerned about how I may have damaged the woman than I am about my money.

Free Association (1)

The twenty bucks suggests payment to a prostitute. Ever since the two-dollar trick went the way of the gold standard, it has seemed to me that twenty bucks should buy a tumble. I'm probably a case of development arrested at the stage when telephones and bus fares were a nickel and a dime bought you the jumbo hot dog. Anyway, the twenty bucks may suggest sex to round out the purchase list of alcohol, tobacco and fucking . . . the bag of vices that must still go together in my unenlightened head, God help me. The business of feeling cheated, not wanting to let her keep the full twenty bucks but yet worrying about being cheap and/or hurting her in her place of work also seems appropriate to the whore background. After all, you don't want to chisel the girl on her established price; on the other hand, you don't feel you've gotten your money's worth; but if you haven't enjoyed yourself enough, whose fault is that? Can the girl be held responsible because you're a creep and couldn't get it up or keep it up, or came too soon? Why do I have to worry about these things in my dreams, too?

The woman in the dream is neither young nor old, neither attractive nor unattractive, not patently sexual. The man who is with me is very dim now in my recall. Certainly, he appears to play no significant role. I am doing the buying; it is my money; it is my complaint about the change. He seems to be merely standing around at my side; perhaps he encourages me to demand the change but nothing more. Certainly, there is a strong feeling about finding the right size package of tobacco, and all I can find at first is the larger package, the tin, which I definitely do not want. I recall that for years I did smoke Edgeworth pipe tobacco and bought both the blue one-pound tins and the small paper packages. In Italy, which all this reminds me of, the problem of getting pipe tobacco was a constant preoccupation. I could go on endlessly with associations about Italy where, incidentally, I saw more prostitutes during those years than in all the rest of my life. Every time you walked the street or drove your car or went to a café, there were girls soliciting; sometimes attractive young girls, too.

Back to the woman .in the dream. She certainly doesn't suggest a hooker. Is she my mother? Seducing me with promises of love and affection, then not delivering, shortchanging me. Yes, that could be my mother in the shop. And how do you complain about getting short-changed by your mother; and to whom do you complain? And don't you worry about what may happen to her if you expose her role in "cheating" you? It may be meaningful that I don't know, in the dream, how much change I should receive. I haven't bothered to ask about any prices.

I only feel certain that the twenty dollars should be more than enough to pay for what I got. Do I discern something phallic in the "bottle" of booze and in the "pipe" tobacco? Well, they have to mean something. We've agreed that there are no meaningless symbols or accidents in dreams. If there is a phallic meaning, is it significant that I definitely reject the large-size "can," "package," and keep looking, not for the smallest, but for the medium size? Am I fighting out again the battle of my father's large cock vs. my small one? Why do I introduce the man friend who has nothing discernible to do in the dream? Is he, perhaps, the doctor (J.N.) who is neutrally watching me squirm in the toils of all these emotional problems, these indecisions, standing back instead of helping me? Am I saying that I expect (in return for my helping him with this project) that he will get into my life and help me?

Manifest Content (2)

The manifest content of the dream is simply that I'm in this shop trying to buy a pouch of tobacco and worrying about getting the change from my twenty dollars. Doesn't seem to tell me much. It's about ten years since I stopped smoking a pipe altogether. Maybe sucking on a pipe had some devastating meaning for me but I recall Freud's oft-quoted crack that "a cigar is still a cigar." I did feel, for years, that I couldn't get along without a pipe in my mouth until I got scared off by fear of mouth cancer. Perhaps my dream is expressing a wish to go back to smoking. But that seems trivial and doesn't conform with any feelings I actually have about smoking now. I really can't find anything interesting in the tobacco aspect of the dream, though it's amusing to consider all this as a "pipe dream." I think my feelings about the twenty dollars and the change I figured I had coming were more important —and my mixed feelings about the woman who stalled about giving me the change. I am worried about money these days; there are people who owe me considerable sums of money and who aren't paying it back. It could well be that the dream is an expression of my anxiety about getting back the money which is owed me in real life. Since this money is lent out to friends who are in difficulty, I really can't press for the return of my money. I am placed in a very awkward position like my position in the dream where I am eager to get the "change" that is due me; yet I am nervous about pressing the lady who's hanging onto my dough (i.e., my friends who are unable or unwilling to return the money they've borrowed). It could very well be that the dream does express just this conflict which nags me in real life. Then, there are all the kibitzers in the cashier's line who express their opinions of the situation. These could very well represent the people in real life who have attitudes, pro and con, about whether I may insist on payment of debts from friends.

Visual and Verbal Clues (3)

I've already discussed such elements as the twenty dollars, the phallic potential of the whiskey and pipe tobacco, the possible identity of the woman in the store and the others who people the dream. Maybe a good punster could make something out of a word like tobacco (go back to?); and the fact that the package of tobacco was so insistently blue. Apart from the fact that that actually was the color of the Edgeworth tobacco I smoked at one time, the color may have emotional overtones; "am I blue"—it's been set to music. Then, there is the really central subject of the dream, the concern over getting my "change." It suddenly occurs to me that "change" may be a very freighted word. Maybe the "change" I'm looking for is not money, but some other kind of change.

In talking with psychologist friends and with J.N., I have been impressed recently with the concept of the mixture and confusion of masculine and feminine identity in most of us; also with the concept that men spend so much energy defending themselves from their normal feminine side that they actually use up some of their masculine energy; so this uptight battle against "femininity" ends up making them less masculine instead of more masculine. Since my own sex life leaves something to be desired (I'm not the stud I'd like to be), I have started to wonder since reading this material whether I haven't fallen into precisely this trap, whether I wouldn't be more relaxed and effective sexually if I gave fuller play to the naturally feminine side of my nature and stopped worrying about being a "sissy" (which tormented me when I was a boy). Yes, this begins to feel right. The "change" I keep worrying about in the dream may very well be a desire for change—of personality—which has developed more strongly than I realized. Perhaps the dream is trying to enlighten me about my need and desire for "change."

Relate Dream to Recent Events—Day Residue (4)

The dream occurred on the night of February 28, the last day of the month. I had been promised some of the money owed to me but the promise had been broken yet again. This left me wondering how I was ever going to collect that money I need. Perhaps this was the "day residue" from which I constructed the dream of wanting the money that was due me. Also, that night there was a bad sex scene for me. My wife and I were making love and it was going quite well. I had no difficulty getting an erection or keeping it; nor any problem about premature ejaculation. Only . . . I couldn't get over the top. I'd pump away to the very point of ejaculation with a full head of steam—then couldn't make it. This is very unusual. I've experienced all other kinds of difficulty from time to time, but never this. It was very frustrating and disturbing. Was this problem connected with the same theme of masculine-feminine identity which has preoccupied me recently? Certainly, if I'm tuning in correctly on the meaning of the "change" concept in the dream, it may very well have been triggered by this disturbing sexual episode.

Identify Cast of Characters (5)

The most vivid character in the dream is the woman in charge of the store, though I can give few details about her physically. I've already speculated that she may be a stand-in for my mother, a woman who "short-changed" me in many ways, being seductive and flirtatious with me on the one hand and withholding her love on the other; overprotecting and "sissifying" me, then shoving me out into the cold world where I didn't know how to cope particularly well; okay, I can see a pattern there that might occur in my dream. I can also speculate that the woman might represent my wife who I have complained for years short-changes me in various departments, especially sex; yet I am afraid to land on her too hard and expose her to others for fear of . . . what? I suppose that I'm afraid if I expose my wife's weaknesses and deficiencies, I will expose my own. After all, I chose her; I've stuck with her for many years; I've always believed that we make our own fate in these matters, that you can't blame a persistently unsatisfactory marriage on the other partner; there's no law that forces people to remain together these days so I can't complain seriously about my wife without directing equally serious criticism at myself. This is a neat enough analogy to what happens in the dream where I feel "cheated" by the woman but somehow feel responsible, myself, for the mess that's been created. After all, I failed to ask the price of the merchandise before I went into the deal, didn't I?

Also, it appears that the woman in the dream can represent the friends who owe me money (not particularly female). So, as it says in the book, the dream symbol can be very compressed and represent much more than a single idea.

More meaningfully, perhaps, as I think about the dream I am more and more persuaded that the vague male companion by my side is the man for whom I am doing this little experiment. The doctor is apparently only interested in me because of this work I am doing for him; he is not bothering to analyze me or take a very passionate interest in me. He's stirred up questions in my mind about my emotional life but he has no intention of intervening to help me. So, in the dream I have him (wishfully?) at my side, not doing much to be sure, but at least supporting me while I demand change from the woman. This dream, then, gives me a chance to tell the doctor that I want and need his attention and help while I fight for that change. This gives the dream another function entirely, a kind of communication or message from me to the doctor. This, I gather, is what happens when a patient brings his dreams in for consideration with his analyst.

Is There Any Overt Sexual Behavior in the Dream? (6)

No.

Is There Any Latent Sexual Content? (7)

I'm told there is *always* latent sexual content, and I've already covered most of the points: the matter of sexual identity (masculine/feminine) as related to the concept of change; my wish to change from a not very effective supermale image to a more relaxed and balanced self-image which admits feminine components and, therefore, permits more masculinity to emerge; the feeling of having been short-changed sexually by both my mother and my wife who both doled out their favors grudgingly; perhaps wrestling with the size of my penis (medium package of pipe tobacco). Evidently, I feel I can't measure up to (or afford) the big can. Whose? It might be my mother who, from the point of view of a child, must have had the big "can." I am certainly determined in the dream not to settle for the smallest package of tobacco. Medium size is what I want; not too big, not too small. By association, this suggests to me the three bears who barged in on Goldilocks. Baby bear was presumably a boy. I don't know if I ever checked that out. But, for sure, the middle bear was a lady bear. Am I trying to tell myself something? Does it have to do with sexual identity or does it mean more simply that I want to go into the shop and get myself a nice comfortable female-like momma bear? At this point, I don't know.

Does the Locale of the Dream Suggest Anything? (8)

As I have remarked, the feeling of the shop in the dream gives me a feeling of Italy, where I lived for years. It's like one of the tourist cafés along the highway that sell local souvenirs, much the same as in this country. There's actually nothing in the dream that specifically suggests Italy or any other country; it just evokes a mood of being on the road in a foreign place rather than close to home. On the other hand, the idea of the shop also suggests my father's workshop back in the garage of our home. I could go on and on about that workshop . . . and I suddenly feel, for the first time, that I should think of the relationship with my father (based on all the time we spent together in that shop) as much more intimate than I have supposed all these years. Certainly, there was constant tension between us. I was always feeling put down. I was bookish, not the ball-playing Frank Merriwell type son he allegedly wanted. But there were good times, too. I can recall learning how to use tools, exciting power tools and learning to make things. I felt useful. And I must have felt that my father was strong, self-sufficient, admirable. It was a physical and masculine world where women seldom ventured. But instead of remembering anything pleasant about the place and about my relationship with my father, I have through the years felt principally resentment and even dislike. For the first time, now, I think of all that as pointless and destructive. What caused these feelings to be so strong that they obscured all the more loving feelings between father and son? Could my mother have been jealous of a possible relationship between my father and me? On what grounds? Did she want both her men competing for her favors? Did she set us at each other's throats? Whatever the roots may have been, I feel now that my shaky masculine identity was based on a distorted picture of what went on between my father and myself. The dream seems to encourage a more mature examination of that all-important workshop of my childhood and of the important feelings that flowed between my father and myself—not just a single set of feelings, but all of them.

What Is the Feeling of the Dream? (9)

Principally, there is a feeling of uncertainty. I'm not sure of my rights; I'm not sure of my right to assert my rights. There is a familiar diffuse anxiety about whether to insist on my position regardless of the consequences to myself or to the lady in attendance. This was not a dream of strong emotion—of terror or excitement. It rather suggests the mood in which I live, turning away from the most potent direct feelings, sensing that they are dangerous and destructive, fearing stronger feelings, protecting myself from pain—at the expense of real commitment. Don't make the pass at the pretty girl; the pain of failure is too unacceptable. Tell yourself it doesn't really matter; you don't really want her; it's better to do without rather than risk rejection. What is the source of this exaggerated fear? What am I actually afraid of? Since I seem to identify with the woman in the shop who may get into trouble for short-changing me, then I appear to be afraid of the authority who "owns" the store. My father? Perhaps. But he's long dead. Why do I go around fearing him and dreaming of his authority? Surely, by now, I've transferred that fear elsewhere. It's "they" who will punish me: the police? . . . the authorities? . . . a jury of my peers? . . . God? What transgressions did I commit when I was young to make me so afraid of punishment? Isn't it true that I have a rather exaggerated sense of how vulnerable I am in this life and so I always hesitate to plunge into action, any action, wholeheartedly? I can't even ask freely and uninhibitedly to get my goddam change from my goddam twenty dollar bill! *Merde!*

Consider the Dream in Series (10)

There was another dream that night, an earlier one from which I woke. I made an effort to remember it and was pleased when I got up in the morning to find that I did. But it is gone now.

The Dream As a Wish (11)

If any of my thinking about this dream is valid, then it appears that I express a number of important wishes in the dream: On a superficial level (manifest content) I am trying to resolve the problem of demanding payment of actual money owed me by friends. On another level, I am making a demand or a plea to the doctor (J.N.) to pay attention to my emotional problems (which he has stirred up with this book) and help me; on still another level, I am trying to face up to my problems of sexual identity and sexual performance; I am saying, in the dream, that some change is in order . . . I must begin to accept the feminine part of me as well as the masculine and this may even turn me into a better-functioning male. As part of this identity problem, I seem to have reached back to my troubled relationship with my father as a key to understanding what plagues me to this day. Finally, there has emerged a strong wish to unburden myself of unrealistic and unproductive fears which interfere grossly with my ability to function with any effectiveness and spontaneity. While I don't yet understand the source of these fears, I think it's healthy that I begin to examine them.

DAN'S SECOND DREAM

I am in a bedroom with C. Both of us are naked on the bed, about to start fucking. I am very surprised when I look at her and find she has a penis (in the usual place), a penis which is large and very much erect. I glance down and compare it with my own which is, if anything, smaller. This worries me a bit but I brush the concern aside in light of my fascinating discovery. My reaction, after my first astonishment, is that this is an opportunity to suck a penis, something which has on occasion struck me as an interesting thing to try. But I have never had the opportunity before. Here, however, is a splendid occasion made to order: a cock on a girl! This will permit me to indulge my curiosity yet take all the homosexual curse off the experience. So, I go over and take it in my mouth. It seems an ordinary enough penis except that it has a kind of conical shape to the tip, a kind of lid, rather like one of those sugar or ketchup dispensers one finds on café tables. In my mouth, I find it is hard, dry, rough, almost like sucking on a dead stick. It is not at all appealing.

Worse, C. reacts furiously to my presumption and insists that I have turned her off completely by this crude behavior. I am surprised and protest that we shouldn't have such strictures; sex is sex. Why make rules about what we can and cannot do so long as we're trying to enjoy ourselves?

Now, we start to make love in the ordinary way Her penis has apparently disappeared but she is hostile and uncooperative. I am having difficulty staying hard. We are now in more familiar territory, alas. I am annoyed with her because she isn't really cooperating. I want her to be more stimulating; to use her hands, grab my ass, pull me into her, participate as a full partner. Instead, she has a passive "show me" attitude and she even goes so far as to ask me if I think I can carry this through to satisfactory completion; otherwise, she'd rather not get worked up only to be let down. This bald attack doesn't help my condition, and I go soft. But I keep trying to overcome her negativism and my own. I evidently succeed quite well, because eventually I am pumping away merrily and feeling much pleasure in her well-lubricated cunt when I awake.

Free Association (1)

Thinking about this dream, I come up with a number of recollections about my childhood. I recall that as an only son I was the apple of my mother's eye but that she gave her love conditionally, snatching it away rudely whenever I did anything to displease her. For example, I recall that when I was only five, I spent a week away from home visiting some rip-roaring cousins who lived in a southside slum where life was lived in the candy store and you damn well ate what you wanted when you wanted, steak for breakfast instead of cereal if there happened to be any meat in the house; you went to the movies and stayed through the show three times until they threw you out and locked the house at midnight; then falling into bed with a boy cousin who was a very mature eight-year-old and explained all about how your mother and father made babies—to your fascinated and unbelieving ears. When I returned home after this glorious week, my mother asked if I had missed her. I casually and honestly said, "No"; she was enraged, pushed me out of her arms and rejected me as a lousy little brat who didn't appreciate or deserve her love.

Not a bad scene for a situation comedy on television, but neither my mother nor I saw the humor at the time. The other side of the rejection was the constant seduction. Mother made me her little man, her private male love, and burdened me with attentions and confidences that were certainly inappropriate. This went on throughout my childhood and was still going on when I was sixteen. At that age, I can recall her telling me that my father had been such an inexperienced and inept lover when they had married that he forced himself on her physically and irritated her vagina to such an extent that she had been unable to urinate and had had to go to a doctor for relief.

I didn't know what to make of such embarrassing confidences but my father was certainly aware, from the beginning, that the other "little man" in the house was the competition. From the start, it had been a bloody battle which I couldn't possibly win. Once, in a rage when I was only four, my father beat me almost senseless for "having a tantrum." The brutal beating had never been repeated but the threat of it seemed to hang over my entire childhood. And, always, my father put me down at athletics and in other ways to prove that I was less of a man than he.

I recall talk about the outsize measurements of my father's penis. It wasn't dinner table conversation but this little pitcher picked up boastful asides about the extra-large condoms which were used; all of which made me feel even tinier. Looking back to those days, it seems to me that the sex pattern at home shook down to this: I wanted my mother with more than normal intensity; she built me up as a male, seduced me, spooned out her love in accordance with how much I served her, but I was scared out of my wits every minute because, for playing the very male role she tempted me with, I was going to have my head beat in (or something worse) by dear old dad.

In adult life, when "real" sex became the game, I couldn't wait to get in there with a woman—all the way, down on her, cunnilingus, back into the womb, no holds barred. But there was always the fear that any real pleasure with a woman would be punished by that father figure in the background who would beat me up, or cut them off, if I really enjoyed myself fucking. Sex became a routine of serving the woman (making damned sure that she came) but robbing myself of true fulfillment.

Manifest Content (2)

Well, this seems to be a dream with enough manifest content for everyone—fucking, sucking, homo, hetero, the works. . . . I'll go along with the notion that there's a homo wish when I suck the cock (and admit in my dream that I've had some interest in that exercise) though I've never actually had any homo experience or any conscious wish for it. So, my dream reveals an unexpected feminine side of me. Of course, I'm not certain that sucking a penis is precisely a feminine trait. By that I mean that a lot of women go through life—and a normal sex life—without ever doing it or, presumably, wishing to do it. But staying with that part of the content of the dream, I find the penis not very appealing. It's rough like a stick or a tree branch: it has a peculiar cap like a piece of hardware. . . . The word, "hardware" rings a bell. It could be a plumbing fitting. Surely, my father was the hardware man, the man who owned and used all the tools in the plumbing shop. This tends to confirm my feeling that the penis in the dream belongs to my father and is strategically located in the girl's crotch to warn me away from the real thing— pussy—on pain of being beaten with a stick by my father. In other words, I see the stick-penis in the dream as a weapon of my father's which always appears threateningly when I want to enjoy myself sexually with a woman.

However, this doesn't explain why I take it into my mouth and even remark in the dream that this is something which had mildly intrigued me, as an idea, from time to time. Maybe I'm being defensive when I hedge this so much but, in all fairness, I can't give the false impression that I've ever been preoccupied with the idea or spent time fantasizing about it. Why suck on it? Why take it into my mouth at all? I'm reminded of certain primitive cannibal rites where the heart of the enemy warrior, or any part of him, is eaten with the idea of incorporating his strength or courage by the act of ingesting his flesh. Perhaps I take the paternal penis into my mouth because I want to be big and strong like daddy or tough and mean and punishing as I conceived him to be when I was young. I may be touching on something real here because I know, in fact, that much as I suffered from my father's aggressiveness and his vituperative side, I have a great deal of all that in me, today. My wife can puncture my nastiness most effectively by remarking that I am behaving very like my father. I recognize how true it is when she says this and I hate myself for it. So, somewhere along the line I learned to emulate the old man. It was probably protective. A little boy sees that his father has it made (he's got mom, money, authority; he's the boss in every way); so, sensibly, the child patterns himself in the same mold. Or, a little boy is pushed around and intimidated by his father and figures he'd better become like that if he wants to be free of fear. He decides he'd be better off on the other side of that equation, better off doing the shoving instead of receiving it.

All of this adds up to the notion that I take my father's penis into my mouth because I want to become my father.

Is there a homosexual aspect to this? Do I want to perform sex with my father as a means of turning his hostility to love? Do I actually feel physical and erotic love for my father? Perhaps, but if so, it must be buried deep where I can't find it.

How about physical and erotic love for my mother? That's hard for me to feel, too—in the sense of really imagining the incestuous adult act between her and me. The thought puts me off. I understand there's a strong incest taboo which works to cover up any feelings which may actually exist; I'm only reporting how I feel. On the other hand, I've always been very oral in my sex. I like to suck titty and anything else I can get my mouth and/or tongue on/in. This reminds me that my mother used to boast of how I loved breast feeding and, later, wouldn't give up bottle feeding until long past the normal age for that. Perhaps, the penis on the woman in the dream is another symbol for my punishing mother and a wish for a giving breast in place of the grudging gratifications she offered in reality. I suppose that both of these concepts (father-penis, mother-breast) can coexist in the same symbol in the compression of a dream.

To go on to another aspect of the manifest content: why does my sex partner in the dream react so furiously when I go down on *her* penis? It seems as if she doesn't consider it hers. If she is a stand-in for my mother, then she may have set up the family triangle in such a way that I would never get close to my father. This made me hers; she didn't have to share me with him; there was no danger of losing me (my love) to him. Considering how jealous she was of my affection, it makes sense that she would try to block my feelings for anyone else, even for my father. Of course, this is my dream. It's not reality we're dealing with. If I say, "My mother set up the triangle . . . etc.," I'm only saying that's how I see it now in my dream. Does such an "insight" conform to reality? I think it may. I think the dream is helping me to see something that has always been there but which I never wanted to understand, i.e., that my mother played an active, if unconscious, role in aggravating the relations between my father and myself. The dream also helps me to see that I may have wanted to emulate my father, to love him and be loved by him, more than I ever appreciated before.

Visual and Verbal Cues (3)

The most striking visual element is the penis which appears to grow out of the girl's vagina, the fact that it feels like a dry stick and has the peculiar cap. I've already covered all that ground. I think my association of the cap with plumbing seems a good clue to the true meaning of the penis.

Relate Dream to Recent Events (Day Residue) (4)

I have recently begun working with a colleague on a major research project in the biology department. For both of us, this is a first effort to do serious and sustained original research which may continue for a period of years and, if successful, produce significant results for our careers. Though the working relationship began in the most positive spirit, there soon developed considerable friction. In a project like this, it is very difficult to proceed without one person who is in command and makes the major decisions. Unwittingly, we fell into an unhealthy competition, a jockeying for control. Instead of collaborating fruitfully as at first, we each began to be overcritical of the other's contribution. This was destructive and disturbing for both of us. We both recognized what was happening, though each of us was convinced that it was the other guy who was really neurotic. But to preserve the project, we each tried to fly right. That's when I had the dream and, unexpectedly, told it to my colleague. I think it was a kind of offering. I was taking this way of saying that I, too, am human; I have my failings; I have my sexual hang-ups; I am not the tough, inflexible, dictatorial type (my father?) you seem to take me for and I'm willing to expose all of this to you as an earnest of my good faith and my desire to continue working together. I suspect that this dream, whatever else it may say about me, my mother, my father and my wife, came along when it did—as clearly as it did—because I needed something like it in my working life. I think it quite likely that the life context in which this dream occurred was a significant motive for the dream.

Identify Cast of Characters (5)

On the face of it, there are only two characters, the girl I am making love to, and myself. Is this really a two-character play or is it more? I think we can forget the one character who represents me because that seems unambiguous enough. But the girl, we have seen from my associations, can also be my mother (grudgingly giving her love), my wife (grudgingly making love) and even my father by virtue of the penis which appears in her crotch. There is still another possibility. Following the self-evident rule that I create all the characters in my own dream, it must be true that I exist in all the characters and so, in part at least, the girl in the dream can be me. After all, she has a cock; and I have a cock—which is something we tend to forget in all this discussion. Does that mean I am going down on myself? Perhaps. But I am intrigued by another doorway opened by the concept that the lady is me.

If I am discovering that the shrill, negative, put-upon girl is me, which of my roles is she playing? We may have to back up a few steps to study this. I did say that my wife sometimes accuses me of emulating my father's worst bullying characteristics. This implies that in relationship to my wife, I relish playing out the reversal of roles from childhood, i.e., I play the bullying father and turn my wife (who else can I bully?) into the small defenseless child (myself). Since I do always choose small women as sex objects, it may be that I relish playing tough daddy to the defenseless child. This throws quite another light on my marriage and on my sex behavior. It suggests that I deliberately set up a configuration where I can resent my wife (or lover), blame her for my sexual dissatisfaction and justify my own antagonistic and rejecting behavior. This would occur because, even more than sexual gratification, what I crave in life is to play the role of the powerful father and thus reassure myself constantly that I am no longer the helpless little victim of my father's anger, rage and punishment. In this light, I can see that the girl in the dream is also myself, provoking me by playing the rejecting feminine and infantile role which inspires and justifies my fatherlike domination and dislike. God knows, when she deliberately demeans me, snidely suggesting that I can't satisfy her, turning me off just when I am starting to enjoy myself, she has earned a kick in the ass. I wouldn't even blame my father for walloping a woman (?) like that.

The behavior of the woman in the dream is also a kind of emasculation of the man and in that sense it suggests an interesting recapitulation of what may have gone on between my mother and father. My mother undoubtedly employed a number of techniques including the use of her darling sonny boy as a club against my father, driving him up the wall and exacerbating all of his hostility. Viewed in this light, as a dream re-creation of the sex scene between my parents, there is reenforcement of the concept that I am identifying with my father, since I place myself in *his* sex role in the dream vis-à-vis my mother.

Getting back to the "cast of characters" in the dream, it now appears that not only can the woman in the dream be my mother, my wife, my father and myself, but even— contrary to my original notion—the character representing me in the dream can also be my father.

Overt Sexual Behavior (6)

There is one other aspect of overt sexual behavior which I haven't touched upon. A point that puzzles me is the relatively upbeat note on which the dream concludes. The fact that at the end I am merrily pumping away as though all my problems are behind me seems false, seems a contradiction of so much else in the dream. If the problems disclosed by this study of the dream exist (and, in fact, the problems do exist), how do I manage to sign off on such a positive note? Perhaps this is merely wishful but I don't often have positive and wishful sexual dreams, so why would I conclude such a disturbing dream as this with a Mary Poppins ending? It may be that precisely because the dream is so rich and revelatory that I am impelled to paper it over with this final bit which, normally, would keep me from examining the entire dream with any seriousness. The "happy ending" may be a mechanism for leading me away from an analysis that opens up such a can of worms, allowing me to continue to stew still longer in my unhappy but comfortable and familiar patterns of behavior.

Latent Sexual Content (7)

This has already been explored in some detail.

Does the Locale Tell Anything? (8)

This dream is without any distinctive locale. Just a bed. I could associate to a lot of beds I have known but I don't know that they would relate particularly to this dream.

Feeling of the Dream (9)

Confusion and inadequacy seem to describe the feelings engendered by the dream, and I have tried to explore some of the sexual correlations to this feeling. It seems equally important to connect such feelings with a more general view of my problems—not merely my life as a son, husband, lover—but as a man who has work and responsibilities in the community. As a university professor, I work in an institutional environment that reflects closely the typical aspects of the society surrounding it (as any large institution reflects the world it serves). There are elements of democracy and of authoritarianism, competition and cooperation, hierarchy and anarchy. Just as I find it difficult to define my sexual role, I have difficulty with my social and professional role. I resent authority but I covet the approval of authority and enjoy power when I have it. This seems to reflect closely the split attitude I carry over from my feelings as a child for my father; and I suppose I want to beat up on the poor university president because to me he'll always be a father surrogate.

More urgently, I feel that I fail to address my energies to constructive work. Instead of doing meaningful original research, I have become a timeserver. The present ambitious research project, mentioned before, is an attempt to break from that pattern but the results are not yet in. I resent all the political maneuvering at the school, refuse to play the departmental games but don't really withdraw from them. I know that the dead hand of bureaucracy rests heavily on the shoulders of all of us who would make a better community between students and teachers but I do nothing effectual to upset the status quo. It seems that the sexual ineffectuality is only one face of a general ineffectuality; it troubles me that my own unsought and unresolved battles from childhood continue to intrude on the real problems of a whole generation of university students. And I suspect, from observing my peers, that my pattern is the rule rather than the exception.

Examine the Dream in Relation to Other Dreams (10)

I cannot connect this dream with any other.

The Dream As a Wish (11)

Do I wish to go down on a man? Perhaps. I have explored that in terms of my need to release and relax the feminine identity in me, an identity which remains imprisoned by the caricature I make of emulating my father's "masculinity." It is necessarily a caricature since my only real impression of my father comes from the child's-eye view I formed at a very early age and it can have very little relation to the real person he was.

Do I wish to fumble and agonize over lovemaking as I do in the middle portion of the dream? I scarcely think so. And I don't need a dream to remind me that inept lovemaking is a painful and demeaning experience. Why, then, do I dream it? What "wish" does that fulfill? Curiously, the midportion of the dream where I go soft functions almost as a transition between the first part where I go down (yield to my feminine side) and the last part where I perform like a male sexual virtuoso. Can I be saying to myself, wishfully, that if I relax about my femininity, I will progress beyond the familiar inadequacy and achieve the sexual prowess I desire?

CHRIS'S DREAM

PERSONAL BACKGROUND:

Chris is a jet-setter who swings both ways. He is one of the rare and enviable people who is able to function creatively as a composer and songwriter, and make a mint doing it. So, he's been around. He's as much at home in London, Paris and New York as in Los Angeles. He's made serious passes at psychoanalysis in almost as many cities and has picked up the language and techniques of the couch. He has been through many sessions of dream analysis and does not have to approach his dreams by the numbers. His technique is more relaxed and natural since, with practice, he has learned to throw away the mechanics and jump right into the feeling of the dream, swiveling from free association to latent content to day residue and so on in any order and then back around again if it seems interesting. Unlike the preceding example (Dan), Chris's approach to a dream approximates the method of the experienced analyst, a no-holds-barred attack that is unrestrained by mechanics. Readers may find this example of Chris at work interesting and illuminating.

Chris's unresolved problem is one of sexual identity. He has a significant homosexual trend and he tends to become homosexual under stress. But he is also capable of loving women and he knows that for him it would be much more gratifying to live with and love a wife and children. He would like to be able to do that with an undivided heart and he pursues this goal in his analysis.

THE DREAM

> I am in northwest Africa, traveling diagonally across the continent with a male companion. I wonder if I should stop to visit Mecca, which seems to be here in northwest Africa. But my problem is that, as a Christian, I may face difficulties in the Moslems' holiest city. But now I am in Mecca; it is a beautiful, tawny, sun-drenched place. Then we proceed to Egypt and are traveling south on the lush, lovely Nile, arriving in Lebanon, which is situated at the Upper Nile—the origin of the Nile. Our final destination is Mombasa, the port city of East Africa. From Mombasa I gaze longingly southeast, yearning deeply to go on to the mysterious Reunion islands of the Indian Ocean. Someone mentions the Union of South Africa, indicating that it is the farthest south one can go in Africa.

I had no difficulty in recalling this dream. It was warm and colorful with many shades, tones and textures. It was adventurous, joyous, filled with discovery and very hopeful. These were the *feelings* of the dream.

I naturally turned my mind first to the exotic African *locale* of the dream which, in this case, clearly flowed from the *day residue*. In the period prior to the dream and, particularly, on the very day preceding the dream, I had been working on an ambitious recording project involving African music. I had been deeply engrossed in this enterprise and had great hopes for a hit record. Very likely I was overly invested emotionally in the project and hoped to

evolve a whole fresh musical style which would answer
the critics who were beginning to dismiss me as warmed-
over rock. Whatever else may have entered my thoughts
in the days preceding this dream, there is no question but
that Africa was a dominant theme.

The *manifest content* of the dream consisted of a trip
across Africa from the northwest to the southeastern portion bordering the Indian Ocean with a number of eccen-
tric geographical details along the way. I was accompanied
by a shadowy male figure. I think that most of us, from the
time of Stanley and Livingstone to the more recent days of
Hemingway and Angola mercenaries, associate Africa with
adventure and exploration. There's little doubt in my
mind that in one sense this traverse of Africa, the Dark
Continent, represented an exploration of my own psyche.
I'm deeply involved in trying to understand my problems,
trying to reexamine, reassess, retrace the years of my life,
treating them as an unknown or half-known territory
which I must explore minutely for the meaning of events,
a meaning that will shed light on all my present attitudes. I
am also feeling restless, bored with the familiar routines,
looking for an exotic escape route from familiar problems.
I realize that this restlessness is a curse; it occurs again and
again when I near the climax of some endeavor, it tempts
me to abandon the work I have done and results in a succession of half-completed and failed undertakings. I
know, too, that this is associated with my central problem
of a search for a more stable sexual identity. So, here I am
again nearing the climax of a project and dreaming of running off to Africa, tempted by the color, rhythm and the
far-offness of that alien continent to abandon my work and
flee to whatever exotic pleasures it has to offer.

The *cast of characters* seems small enough. In addition to
myself, there is only the shadowy male companion who
seems to go along with me the whole time and the even
less substantial person who, at the end, remarks about the
Union of South Africa. Of course, I've been over this kind
of ground before; when I encounter a vague male figure in

my dream, I've learned to think in terms of my father, my analyst and any other father substitutes I've known, authoritative males with whom I have worked or played. Since this is such a warm dream, I think of the male companion as the "good" part of my father and all the other good fathers in my experience. Perhaps, as well, it is the much desired male part of myself, accompanying me on this interesting journey. Certainly, that's the positive way to approach the otherwise unidentified figure. However, I've been dreaming a long time and looking into my dreams; I know that they're rarely simple, clear, wish-fulfillment exercises; they're usually complex and, above all, ambivalent. So, I must consider the possibility that I am accompanied on this fanciful tour by the ever-present shadowy curse of homosexual longing which continues to plague me no matter how much I want it to be otherwise.

The *visual and verbal cues* in this dream are really amusing and imaginative if I say so myself: a beautiful holy city in the desert; a lush tropical river; the marvelously inviting islands of the warm Indian Ocean. Verbally, there are names like Mecca, Lebanon, Mombasa. These will certainly yield some interesting free associations.

There is no *overt sexual behavior* but the dream is fairly dripping with *latent sexual content* which will certainly develop with free association.

My *free associations* frequently come first when I think about a dream, tumbling out impatiently even as I am trying to recall the dream and set it into words. At other times, like now, I enjoy playing around with elements like the identity of the characters, the locale, the feeling, the day residue, before I settle in for the revelations that usually come with the free association: Africa seemed so dusky, sensual, so wrapped in its own special luminousness that was soft and yet could coexist with the harsh sandy desert. It was mostly sunlight. The dream was a beautiful journey that seemed to repeat circumstances and discoveries from my early life and also contained promises of further discoveries in my present adult life. When I was a child, I visited Africa with my father and mother. It was a wildly exciting time, a genuine big game safari; it was frightening, thrilling and darkly moving in ways I still don't understand. It was a real experience but in my mind it has the overtones of a dream remembered from another life. It's curious how hazy the details of that time have become; what I recall most clearly comes from a photograph we have at home, a photo of me as a slim, dark-eyed child, almost girlish-looking, standing beside a lion my father had shot. I am holding the huge rifle which is almost as large as I. Did my father really shoot the lion? Yes, he is capable of that kind of brutality. How I wish he had been warmer, more loving.

But now that I am back to Africa in my dreams, I am no longer that slight, delicate boy; I am heavier and my features are coarser, things I don't really like, yet they mean that I am more man. As I ponder the meaning of this, a pun from the dream makes me smile: Mecca is like pecker. Mecca is a holy city, a city of mosques and minarets. Can anyone who has ever seen a minaret doubt that it is a giant penis thrusting erect from the earth into the sun-bleached skies? Now, I am a tiny hummingbird, hovering around the top of the minaret, futilely trying to suck at the huge dome which has become the beautifully rounded tip of a penis. Who do the Arabs think they're kidding? The minaret is my father's penis; he is back in Africa with me again; and the sandy flesh-colored city that sprawls below is the body of my father.

But I know I can never satisfy this gigantic penis and how could I ever compete with it? I must turn in another direction. I turn to the Nile, that great feminine symbol, a mother of civilizations, a fertilizer of the desert, a mouth into the darkness of central Africa. The Nile is Cleopatra, the female goddess of antiquity, periodically overflowing and renewing the life of this ancient land. I love this female thing and want to lose myself in it. Through Lebanon? Of course, Lebanon equals labia, the lips, the entry into a woman's sexual organs. I think of the Nile again as it moves imperceptibly but imperturbably through the desert, serene as I once saw it on a blazing summer afternoon, the only place of refuge in the burning wasteland near the Valley of the Kings. The river is so level, so broad, so safe and, suddenly, so erotic. I begin to feel aroused; I get an erection, and I want to bury myself deeply, totally in the body of a beautiful woman.

My sexual feelings make me anxious, and I see myself as a crocodile, eyes and snout breaking the surface as I float up the river. My face reaches Mombasa . . . momma . . . mother. I am very happy. I am still facing southeast and I want to go on to the Reunion islands off the coast of Africa, islands that rise from the sea are her breasts which I want to reach out to. And, most of all, I want to bathe in the deep warm blue of the Indian Ocean, immerse myself in that magical fluid that is my mother's.

Yes, I want someone with whom I can join my life. I'm tired of the transient liaisons, the one-night stands, the pickups; I'm angry at the thought that I am still bound to this kind of love. In the dream I was happy because I had a companion always at my side, a man, a father, a father substitute. But I will never be able to please my father any more than that tiny hummingbird could satisfy the minaret. Besides, I want to be with a woman, not a man. At this point, I feel that the only way I will be really happy is if I can marry a woman I love. I know that in the dream I have been exploring many things, not least of them the feelings I have had for both my father and mother. I journeyed over the bodies of both of them in the dream and with great pleasure as well as frustration and apprehension. In the past I was never able to relate so intimately to my parents, even in a dream. I feel this dream is a watershed; of course, I want it to be. But it is true that I seem to be rediscovering my love for both my parents and in this way I can rediscover my love for myself. I know that only through learning to love myself in the right way, instead of hating myself, disliking and depreciating myself, can I achieve mature love, lasting meaningful love for another person.

By now it is clear, as usual, that the *cast of characters* is larger than it initially appeared to be. We have a hummingbird (which is me) and a crocodile (which is me), a phallic cock-minaret (which is my father and also me); my father is there and also my mother and, of course, I am present in all. In my associations I am also present as a slight, girlish twelve-year-old standing beside the freshly killed lion, a child who is fearful of growing into a heavy-featured man. Am I also the heavy-featured lion who was shot down by my father? I begin to see in this dream a connection between my childhood and my adulthood; in the years since that photo was made, I have not matured as much as I should; I still carry about inside me too much of that tentative child and feel about things much the way he felt. There is an unbroken continuity which should be broken; I am still the child who stands beside the lion which someone else shot. I am not yet prepared to shoot the lion myself.

THE AUTHORS' COMMENT

Chris is struggling earnestly with the problem of sexual identity. The dream and its associations are a battleground of homosexuality vs. heterosexuality, of love for father vs. love for mother; it is rich ground for the reexamination of immature attitudes that persist into the present. The dream fulfills Chris's wish to live a heterosexual life; he becomes aroused at the thoughts of sex with an attractive female while responding to the feminine suggestion of the river in the dream. More, the dream is wishful in the sense that it satisfies his need to experience the different facets of his sexuality, a kind of psychodrama in which he can play out and evaluate different roles.

Note that Chris is undaunted by absurdity, which is characteristic of *every* dream. Mecca has been moved, somehow, from Saudia Arabia to the western part of Africa; and Lebanon has been moved deep into the heart of the continent. Chris, like any experienced dreamer, welcomes the distortions of time, place and person which characterize dreams. If a dream is too close to reality, its tight logical organization may render it more difficult for the dreamer to analyze. On the other hand, when a dream is loosely organized, full of absurdities and contradictions and with strong feelings of sensuality or sexuality, the dreamer remains unburdened of rational or linear progression; he can use symbols, words, images, feelings as a leaping-off place for plunges into the depths of his history and experience, making contact with the truer feelings which must be retrieved from the hidden deeps where they resist discovery.

Chris has learned to be open, absorptive; he doesn't reject unguarded and uncensored ideas that leap to mind; he allows them to roam freely around in his head, waiting for those which have vitality and authenticity, ideas and concepts that ring a bell. This is what Freud called free association. Puns are very important: Mecca equals pecker; Lebanon means labia; Mombasa stands for momma. These aren't funny puns but they bring insight to the dreamer. Africa, itself, is a symbol and Chris readily apprehends that his dream is a journey to find light on the Dark Continent, i.e., a quest for self-knowledge through the thickets of his unconscious. Light and dark. The interplay of opposites is very common in dreams; thus, Africa is both bright and dusky. Consistency may plague petty minds; it never plagues the dreamer; perhaps it is not too much to say that the mind is working at its freest, at its least small and limited level when it is busy dreaming.

Eventually the dream analysis must stop. Sometimes, a single simple meaning is the essential result of the study. At other times, as in this dream, there are a number of related, overlapping conflicting psychological themes. It is not a tidy package; it is more like a heavily laden table, groaning under a splendid abundance of food for the mind.

Caveat Lector

I am a man; and nothing human is foreign to me.
· TERENCE ·

This book was designed for people who are interested in dreams in general, sexual dreams in particular and their own dreams above all.

It would exceed our hopes—and fears—it would certainly exceed our intentions if, as a result of reading this book, anyone were to consider himself a dream analyst. But we hope the reader will have been stimulated to recall his dreams more vividly, to think and feel about his dreams more deeply and to weave his dreams more creatively into the fabric of his ongoing psychological life.

What matters, finally, is not to master all the answers (no one does) but to master the art of growth. If you glean some truth from each of the dreams you recall, you will be growing and stretching yourself. This is the best part of the human condition.